ANGEL NUMBER 3032

The characters and events in this book
are fictitious . Any similarity to real
persons, living or dead is coincidental
and not intended by the author.

TABLE OF CONTENTS

1

GOODBYE BILL

My shift was almost over. Fifteen hours and counting, and three more hours to go. As a nurse, you feel like that is all you do. Work…. I didn't care. I didn't have too much to look forward to when I got home. A husband that didn't care about me. A husband that swore at me and treated me like shit. He was always drunk. He threw things at me and beat me.   He went to work, but came home and got drunk every single day. He did nothing around the house to help. He wouldn't even take the garbage out. Our neighbors hated him and the kids stayed away from our house. I have put up with this shit for 8 years. I felt like I was trapped with him. I needed to get away. I needed him out of my house. It WAS my house. He just moved in when we got married. It was fully paid for when we got married, so he decided he would move in with me because he was renting an apartment. I didn't know where to start. Plus, I was scared. I had friends at work, but didn't really know who I could trust without the information traveling through my whole department. There was only one girl that I talked to almost everyday. Her name was Stephanie. Maybe I could ask her if she knew anything about divorce and how to proceed? I did some googling on the subject but everything is so vague.

We did not have any children. We tried, but nothing ever happened and now there was no sex because he was always passed out and if he wasn't, he was screaming obscenities at me. My gynecologist said it wasn't me, so it had to be him. He wouldn't go get tested so we just left it at that. Actually, now I am glad we didn't have children together. He turned out to be such an asshole.

I am 30 years old and my name is Margaret (Meg or Meeg) Finley. I am from the Scottish decent. My married name is Mason. My husbands name is William (Bill). He is 33. He is from the French decent.

We lived in Kingsport, Tennessee. It is a growing town in Tennessee in Sullivan County. It has a lot of local shows, restaurants and overall it is a great place to live. Kingsport is home to several high-quality healthcare facilities, which is why I bought here to be close to my job at Holston Valley Medical Center. Kingsport has 15 State Parks, 5 National Parks and 6 different lakes. If you like the outdoors, this is the best place for you. I live on Periwinkle Place in the higher numbers. The lower numbers were condos.   It was a 2 bedroom, 2.5 bath house with 2,594 sq ft. The houses on Periwinkle were exquisite. Whoever the builder was, had good taste.

I lived with my Grandma, on my mom's side, until I was almost 20. My mom and dad died in a car accident when I was 12 and she took me in and cared for me. My Mom and Dad had a trust for me, so when I was 18, I was able to collect it. My grandma had to sell their house and everything they owned and this was my trust. I can't imagine having to do this for your deceased daughter. It must have been so hard for her. My grandpa died before this happened, so she was on her own with me. I love my Grandma with all my heart and soul and I would do anything for her. Anything. I went to nursing school when I graduated high school and she wanted me to stay with her while I was doing that. She said it would be easier on me and it was. I used some of the money from the trust so I wouldn't have any student loans. They left me a lot. I knew when I became a nurse, I would be making good money and I wanted to put a chunk of money down on a house so I could afford the mortgage payments and still have a good chunk of money in the bank.

Bill never gave me a cent towards the mortgage and his name was NOT on my house so it shouldn't be a problem when we split up. He never even paid a single electricity or heating bill. He paid for nothing. All his money was his and he drank it all.   I had my Grandma put the rest of my money in her safe, so it was hidden. I wasn't sharing that with any drunk and he never knew about it. I knew he would try something, like trying to take half of my house, but I would fight tooth and nail before he did that to me. This was MINE and MINE only. And I wouldn't even have it, if my parents were alive.

I was so unhappy living like this. I had to do something quick. Like yesterday. I wanted him out. I got home from work and there he was sitting in the living room on my recliner with a bottle of whiskey in one hand and the TV remote in the other. I told him I was sick of this shit and that started a fight, like I knew it would. He threw the bottle at me and I ducked and it hit the wall. He came at me and I kicked him in the balls. I yelled at him, "GET THE FUCK OUT OF MY HOUSE AND DON'T COME BACK". He rolled around on the floor groaning in pain. I told him to get up and get out. He kept rolling around. I called the police and told them there was a fight and that he threw a bottle at me and I wanted him out. They came. They tried to talk to him, but he was too drunk. They saw the hole in the wall and the broken glass and whiskey everywhere. I told the cop I did not want him back in this house and that I was going to file for divorce. He told me to file a restraining order against him and told me what to do. I gave him my statement and he chuckled when I told him that I kicked him in the balls. I asked if he knew if he could take half of my house and I explained my situation. "He could try, but I doubt he will get anywhere with that. Get yourself a good lawyer honey". They put him in handcuffs and dragged him to the police car. I called my Grandma and told her what I did. "I wondered how long it would take you to get rid of that piece of shit Meeg". My Grandma was the only one that called me that. Everyone else called me Meg or Meggie. She was happy. I told her I was going to file a restraining order and I had to get going so I could get that done. She said, "Pick me up. I will go with you". She was a very smart woman and I looked up to her. I said, "OK, Grams, I will be there in 10 minutes. I got out of my nurses uniform and got my jeans and a T-shirt on and went to pick up my Grams and we both went to file the restraining order.

She knew a lot about this kind of stuff and I never knew how. I asked her how. She said, "Oh, you didn't know that back in MY day" and she started laughing, "I was a senior paralegal. I know my stuff young lady. You just ask me and I will tell you everything to do". I was stunned. "Really Grams? That is very impressive. How come I didn't know about this?". We got to the police station and I told them what I wanted. The Sergeant at the desk got me the form and Grams was pointing here and there. "Fill this and this and sign here." The Sergeant was looking at her and he was impressed. He never said anything, but he was smiling at her. He knew she knew her stuff. So it was done. I filed the fucking restraining order and now he couldn't come back. I said, "Come on Grams, I need to get some boxes, so I can pack his shit. He is OUT of there". I asked her if he could take half of my house and she said, "Remember when were at the closing and I asked the attorney for a quitclaim deed? I made that stupid shit sign it. He can't do a God Damn thing. I didn't tell him what he was signing and he was too stupid and drunk to know.   It's in my safe with the rest of your trust. I put the money back into a trust, so no one could take it on you." See, this is why I love my Grandma so much. She is always watching out for me. Grams told me that the only thing he was getting were the clothes in the boxes that would be waiting for him. She said she would go with me to file for the divorce. "It should be easy, Meeg. He doesn't own anything and has no claims to anything and no kids. Thank the Good Lord".

I asked my boss for a week off and told her what I was doing. She gave it to me and gave me a high five. She knew some of what I was going thru. I came to work with covered up black eyes and bruises. Yes, I was beat up, but too afraid to do anything. She took pictures of me when I came in that way and she just said it would come in handy some day. She used to tell me all the time to get rid of him. She handed me an envelope and told me to use it in court. It was all the pictures she took of me when I came in black and blue and bruised. Why the hell did I wait so long? What is wrong with me? I don't think my Grams knew about this. I never told her but she may have seen the bruises and didn't say anything to me. She always minded her business, unless I was in danger.

I finally told my friend at work, Stephanie. I asked her to please not say anything to anyone and she said she wouldn't, but everyone knew there was something going on. She said she saw some of my bruises but didn't want to interfere. She said, "I will take the rest of the day off. Let me come with you and help you pack his shit. I can help you deal with some other stuff that may come up". I didn't know what she meant by that but I invited her back to my house to help me.

We got to the house and I ordered a pizza and some salads so we could eat lunch. We sat and ate lunch together. We did that at work too. She was a really good listener. I told her what happened the other night and showed her the hole in my wall. She told me that her brother was in construction and she would have him come over and patch it up for me. She texted him right then and there and he said he would come tomorrow. Wow. That was super nice

of him. I told her how much I appreciated that. She said,
"This is the last thing you need to worry about, with
everything else on your plate. I am glad we can help you".
And then she said, "Meg, can I ask you a question?" I said,
"Yes". She said, "It's none of my business, so you don't
have to answer if you don't want to, but why did you wait
so long to get rid of him? He beat you up so many times.
You know he can be arrested for that? Your life was in
danger girlfriend." I told her that I was afraid. I didn't know
how to go about it and I didn't want him to take my house
away from me. She said, "I wish you confided in me a long
time ago, I would have helped you. I am here to help you
now". I started crying. I knew it was coming. I have been
tearing up all day and just holding it back. "I WAS SCARED
STEPH. SO SCARED OF WHAT HE WOULD DO TO ME".
She assured me he wouldn't be doing anything to me
anymore and that I did the right thing by filing the
restraining order. "He has to have a cop escort him in here
to get his boxes. He can't just come and get them now
because of the order. Let's get packing". We went upstairs
and we emptied out his dresser and closet. All his shoes
and sneakers, his one pair of work boots, his one suit and a
couple of dress shirts. All the rest were jeans and t-shirts.
He had a box of razors and shower stuff. He had a few
personal things on top of his dresser. I looked everywhere
to make sure all his stuff was out. He had a few things in
the garage. A fishing pole and a tackle box, a pair of skis
and his fucking piece of shit car. Stephanie said, "Let's
pack up his car and then he can just get in it and drive
away". So we lugged all the boxes downstairs and loaded

up his trunk and backseat and we fit everything in from the garage. I backed his car out of the garage and moved mine in. That was always a fight too. He felt that he should be the one to park in the garage and my car should stay out because I left first and came home last. Now he can kiss my ass. The car would stay out there till he came to get it. I knew I would be getting a call that he was coming for his stuff and it happened 2 days after he went to the drunk tank in jail.   I told the cops that I packed up everything he owned and put it in his car and I would bring my key out when they got here. Bill told the cop that he had stuff in the house and wanted to come in. The cop said I had to let him as long as he was there. I didn't want any problems, so I let him. I followed them upstairs to make sure he didn't take anything of mine. He was fiddling around with the mattress on our bed. "WHAT ARE YOU DOING THERE?" I said. The cop went around to the side he was on and lifted up the top of the mattress and what do you know.? He tried to plant some cocaine in there in a baggy. Fucking dirtbag. Where the hell did he get that from? The cop slapped the cuffs on him again. I told the cop that I did not want him back in the house and that all his stuff was packed in boxes and everything he owned was in his car in the driveway and that I wanted it gone. He said they would send a tow truck to get it. The cop put a pair of gloves on and took the cocaine and put it in a bag. I dangled the keys in front of asshole. "BUH BYE SHIT HEAD".

I told my boss and Stephanie what happened when I was out of work. My boss said, "It's a good god damn thing that you were watching him".   This whole thing is way worse than I thought in the beginning. He really was a piece of shit and he was going to try to take me down with him.

I called my Grams to let her know about the shit he tried to pull, right in front of the cop. He knew the cop wasn't paying attention to what he was doing. He knew the cop was just there to protect me from him. This made my Grams furious. "Well, he had nothing and now he has less than that." She asked if I wanted to come and stay with her and I told her that I wanted to stay here and protect my house, but that she could come and stay if she wanted. She said, "Nah, but thanks for asking Meeg. Make sure you put your alarm on all the time". I told her my windows and doors were locked and the alarm was even on when I was home. I asked my Grams if I could take my old name back when I got the divorce and she said, "Absolutely. I will show you where to put that. Get the papers and I will help you".

Grams came with me to the court and we met with a woman who helped people fill out the papers and gave them advice. I put FINLEY in the space provided and I would get my name back when this was over. I had the envelope of pictures in my purse. "Grams, I have something to show you, but I don't want you to get upset". I told the woman that I had evidence of physical abuse. Grams looked at the pictures and started crying. "I knew it. I knew he was doing that to you". She handed the woman the pictures and the woman looked horrified at me.

"Honey, how long has this been going on?" I told her I was too scared that he might do something else to me if I reported him. I told her my boss took the pictures and just gave them to me when I told her I was filing for divorce. "It's been a couple of years now". She made copies of them and handed me the originals and told me to give them to my lawyer. "Get a lawyer hon and put this guy behind bars". She recommended a few lawyers to me. I was looking at the names and Grams was looking and pointed to one. "This one hon. I know him. I worked for him. He will help you. When we get home, I will call him for you, ok?" I agreed and thanked the lady for her help. She said she would file the paperwork and my attorney could file an appearance for me.

I felt like a boulder just fell off my shoulder. I got in the car and just sighed. Then the tears came again. Not sad tears. Tears of relief. Good tears. Grams gave me a hug. "This shouldn't take long and he will be history". She called Attorney Benson when we got home and they caught up a little before she told my story. He agreed to meet with me at my house the next day and said he would be here after lunch.

Grams came to my house for lunch and we sat and had a sandwich and chips before the attorney showed up. She said, "You are going to be fine. Just be normal. He is a nice guy". I told her I wasn't nervous at all. I think because she knew him.

He showed up. He was an older gentleman about 55-60 and dressed in a nice suit and tie. He was very friendly and he looked very professional. I made him a cup of coffee and he asked me tons of questions. I gave him the pictures and he raised his eyebrows. "This guy is not only going to be divorced, he will be behind bars for a while. I will represent you. And don't worry, he is not getting anything from you. Are you sure you don't want his clothes?" He was laughing. Grams gave him a copy of the QuitClaim and he put that in my file. Attorney Benson looked at my Grams and said, "Good Thinking, Louise". Louise was my Grams name. Grams was not only smart as a whip, but she was funny. "I knew he was an idiot". I looked at her. "Why didn't you say anything to me Grams?" She said, "Because people that are in love don't see what other people see on the outside". I shook my head.

Attorney Benson filed his appearance in my case and he took care of everything. I should have done this years ago instead of suffering and being unhappy. I wasted so much of my life with this asshole. Four months later, Bill and I were divorced. We had to fill out a bunch of forms for the court. He wanted support from me. LOL. No way Jose!. Attorney Benson showed the Judge the pictures of the physical abuse that I endured and Bill got nothing, nada, zilch, zero. The Judge was also informed of him trying to hide cocaine under my mattress and the cop came to testify. He walked away with his car and his clothes and he was forbidden to come near me or my house. I walked away from the Court with my Grams and my attorney and I was so fucking happy to be rid of him. I had my old name back. "Margaret Finley". I said it out loud. Grams tried to pay Attorney Benson, but he wouldn't take it. He thanked her for her years of service to him and said he owed it to her to help. I thanked him and asked him if I could at least take him out to dinner, but he refused and said it was his pleasure to help me. He got in his car and waved to us. I hugged my Grams and thanked her for helping me get rid of him. She said, "He was an idiot and a leach and now he is gone.

2

BACKYARD FRIEND

Move on with your life Meegs. Find a man that is smart like you and a man that will love you and take care of you and don't look in a bar for him". She started laughing. I told her that wouldn't happen.   I took Grams out for dinner to her favorite place, Maple Creek Bistro. She ordered the Maple Creek Burger and Baked Potato. I got the Red Shrimp and Grits and I let her taste it. She loved it so much that she said she would order next time.

I walked into my house and sat on my couch and sunk into it. What a relief! I was happy, but tired. I turned on my speakers and played some of my music from my playlists. I got up and changed my clothes and got into some sweat-shorts. I cut them off and did the same to the sweatshirt. I made it a midriff top and cut the sleeves off. I walked out on my front porch and the lady across the street was sitting on her porch and my next door neighbor was standing in her grass getting her mail. I shouted at the top of my lungs and I didn't care what people thought. "HE IS FUCKING GONE. I GOT RID OF HIM. I AM DIVORCED".   The lady across the street started clapping and said, "Took you long enough lady. Congratulations".   The lady next door said,

"Ah that is wonderful. I am happy for you and for the neighborhood." I walked back in my house and I can't tell you the feeling that came over me. I was overwhelmed with happiness. I can do anything I want now without listening to that fucking pain in my ass. I started dancing in my living room to the music that was playing. Maybe I will have some neighbors that will like me now.

I called Stephanie to let her know it was a done deal and that he got nothing. She asked if I wanted to go out to celebrate. I said, "At a bar? No thanks. Not interested in meeting anyone from a bar". And I laughed. She did too. "Yeah, so where do you go to celebrate?" I told her I would celebrate at home. "You like margaritas Steph?" She said, "Oh hell yeah". I told her to come over in an hour. I had to go get some stuff to make them. She said, "Fuck that, I will bring what we will need to make them and I am coming now. Ya. HOOOO. I am so happy for you".

Steph came over and she hugged me as she came in the door with her bag of celebratory booze. She had the biggest smile on her face. My music was still playing and I turned it up a bit. It was party time. We were in the kitchen making margaritas. She brought Tostitos and Salsa and I put them out on the coffee table. She started dancing around my living room and I joined her. We sipped Margaritas and had Tostitos and Salsa and danced to music and had so much fucking fun. I needed this so bad. She was fun to be with. I never did this with her before. We just hung around at our job and ate lunch together. I had no idea how much fun she would be. We partied until midnight and she left to go home and I told her we needed to do this on a regular basis. She said, "Next time, my house, next Friday night at 6:00 and we will have dinner first". I hugged her and thanked her for helping me celebrate and a good time. "Sure thing girl. I had a great time". I cleaned up and headed into bed.

I slept until 9:00 a.m. I heard birds singing outside and dogs barking and people talking next-door. I got up, put on my robe and made myself a coffee and I walked out onto my deck and plopped in one of my cushioned chairs to sip my coffee. I was never able to do this either. He would say, "People will see you out there with your robe on. Stay inside".   You know what I say now? "Fuck those who don't like it. I am sitting out here in my robe to sip my coffee and I will continue to do this for the rest of my life and those who don't like it can go fuck off". And guess what? No one saw me and no one said anything at all. It was pretty private out here anyway. I had trees surrounding that side of my house. I enjoyed that cup of coffee so much. I went inside to make myself another cup. I made myself a couple eggs and a slice of toast and took it out on my deck and put it on the table and ate my breakfast out there too. I felt like a free person again. I was sipping my second cup of coffee when I heard a man say, "Good Morning Meg. Haven't seen you out here in a long time. It was the man who lived behind me. He was about my age. He had brown hair and brown eyes. He was tall and slender and he was very good looking. I think he was married but I wasn't sure. I have always liked him and I was attracted to him.   I said, "Good Morning Charlie. How are you?". He told me he was good and said, while laughing, "Where's Bill, did you bury him out here in the garden?" I laughed with him and pointed to my garden. "Yup right there. Actually I divorced the son-of-a-bitch. I couldn't take his shit anymore". He looked shocked. "Really? Wow, I guess that's a good thing. I never met anyone as miserable as that man, ever. What took you so long?" I told him what happened in a shorter story and he told me I looked happy and I told him I have never been happier. "How is your wife, Charlie?" He looked at me puzzled. "Meg, I am not married. Never have been married". I guess I got my answer. "Oh, Charlie, I am so sorry. I don't know why, I just always thought you were married. I guess I shouldn't have assumed". He laughed and said, "Yeah, you know what they say about assuming". He started walking towards his house. I yelled. "HAVE A GOOD DAY CHARLIE, SEE YA AROUND". He turned around and said, "You too." He stopped walking, turned around and said, "Maybe someday I can take you to lunch?" I told him I would let him know. "I am not really ready to date anyone right now. It has been a rough 8 years with that asshole". He laughed and said he would keep in touch and I said ok.

I took my dishes and cup inside and rinsed them and put them in the dishwasher. I stepped into the shower and enjoyed the hot water. I no longer had a timer to take a shower. Oh yeah... He really was a bastard. I couldn't take any longer than 10 minutes or he wouldn't have enough hot water to take his fucking 40 minute shower. I took the longest shower and enjoyed every minute. Got out and got dressed and put on my sneakers. I was going to go for a walk. My first walk in 8 years. I was going to walk around my neighborhood and I was going to talk to people. Nope, I was not allowed to do this either. Why the hell did I listen to this guy and do what he said? He was so bossy and demanding and I let him. I had the nicest walk and talked to people along the way and then went home. I took my shoes off before walking in. I decided to do a little cleaning so I wouldn't have to do it on Sunday. I made my bed and I dusted all my furniture and took out the vacuum and did all my floors. I got my mop and did my kitchen and bathroom floors. I spruced up my bathroom. I washed down my kitchen counters and stove and sprayed my appliances with windex and cleaned those up. I changed all my towels, kitchen and bathroom and put a load of laundry in the washer. I started the dishwasher. Voila! All clean and now I was going to go grocery shopping for a few things and I had an envelope to mail, so that would go in the mailbox on my way out. When I came back, I put all the groceries away, emptied the dishwasher and put the clothes in the dryer that I washed earlier. All I had left to do chore wise, was fold the clothes and put them away.

I called Grams to check in on her and she was happy to hear from me. I told her how I celebrated with Stephanie on Friday night and that I did my cleaning, shopping and laundry already. "What are you doing tomorrow Grams? Do you have any plans?" She was so funny. "Well, I don't know, let me check my calendar honey". She was silent for a second and then started laughing. "Um, no I don't see anything for tomorrow. What are you thinking?" I asked her if she would like to go out for dinner and a movie. She said, "It's a date. I would love that sweetheart". I told her I would pick her up at 4:00 p.m. I did this a lot because my Grams means a lot to me. She is my everything. She always has been and she always will be. She was always there for me, my whole life. Now it's my turn to show her how much I appreciated her and loved her. I made it a point to take her out at least once a week. If I couldn't do it on the weekend, I would do it during the week after work. Even if it was to MacDonalds, I still took her out. This was another thing asshole didn't like. I used to tell him, "Tough shit Bill. This woman took care of me from when I was 12. She is my mom, my dad and my grandma, all in one and I will take her out once a week, whether you like it or not". That is one thing I always stuck to and he was not going to change that. My Gramma knew it too. She knew he gave me a hard time, every weekend and she used to say, "Tell him I said, go to hell". She knew I had to argue every weekend to do this with her and I told her I didn't care because I was doing it anyway. I told her, "You are my gramma, my only family and I will keep coming to take you out, no matter what". I knew she appreciated it. She didn't have to say anything. She was alone all week, except for her neighbor friends. She used to play cards once a week with them.

I relaxed in front of the TV for the rest of the afternoon. I made myself a salad and some ravioli with a piece of garlic bread and opened a coke, for supper and I ate it on my deck. I saw Charlie in the back watering his garden and that reminded me that I should do that too. I will get to it after supper. I might have some veggies out there that are ready. Charlie saw me and waved and I waved back. I finished my dinner and brought everything inside and cleaned up. I went out back with my hose and started watering my garden. Charlie was still out doing his. He nodded his head at me and I said, "You reminded me that I didn't do this today". He said, "Glad I could help you out". I felt bad because earlier I was kind of rude to him so I asked him, "Would you like to come over for a cup of coffee with me?". He smiled at me and said, "Um yeah, I would love that. I'll be over in a few minutes". I finished watering and went back to the house. I dried off because I got spattered with water from the hose. He came to my side door and knocked because I had the storm door open. "Come in Charlie". I pointed to the coffee selection and asked, "What kind would you like?" He said, "Regular is just fine". I made him a regular and I had a decaf. I had a tin of butter cookies and I handed him the tin, "Can you bring these outside?" I carried the coffee's and he held the door for me. I told him that I almost forgot to water and I thanked him again for reminding me. He just laughed. "How are your veggies doing?" He asked. I told him I had some ready, but didn't have time to pick them. He said, "Oh, when we finish, I can help you pick them and bring them back to the house, if you want". I agreed and said, "Thanks". He was staring at me and said, "So you got rid of him. Can I ask you a personal question?" I said, "Yes". He was a little hesitant and then said, "Meg, did he hurt you, like did he physically hurt you?" I told him that he did for many years, but I was afraid to do anything. He told me that he heard the fights and me screaming in pain and crying. He told me he wanted to barge in and beat the shit out of him for hurting me. "I kind of knew it, and it was killing me. Now I am sorry I didn't barge in". I told him I was fine and I was happy now. I told him there were so many things that he wouldn't let me do (in my own house). I started telling him about my timed showers, how I couldn't listen to my music, I wasn't allowed to take a walk in the neighborhood, I couldn't dance, I couldn't change out of my nurse's uniform before making him dinner. I had to come right home and not allowed to stop anywhere and had to start cooking immediately. He looked horrified at what I was telling him. "OMG, you were a prisoner in your own house. How did you cope with this shit for so long? Why did you let him get away with this shit?" I told him that I was afraid of him and that when I talked back to him, he would swat me or punch me or kick me, so I let him boss me around. We talked for a while about that and then I asked him to change the subject and to tell me about himself. We took the coffee cups and cookie tin inside and he said, "Let's go pick your veggies. Do you have something to put them in?" I told him there was box in the garage that I used so he went out to get it. We walked down to the garden and we were talking while picking veggies. I had a ton of peppers ready. I had green, red, purple and also Cubanelle peppers ready. I had cherry tomatoes and Campari tomatoes ready. I had cucumbers ready and I had zucchini and yellow squash ready too. We filled the box. I asked him if he needed anything. He took a couple of cucumbers and Cubanelle Peppers and he told me what he had and he said he would bring me a watermelon and a spaghetti squash. We talked about some recipes that we made from our gardens and we shared a couple. He carried the box back to the house for me. It was pretty heavy and I wouldn't have been able to do it. I would have had to get my wheelbarrow. I thanked him for his help and he went home.

3

NOT A DATE

I woke up Sunday morning around 8:00 a.m. I showered, got dressed, put on my makeup, brushed my teeth, brushed my hair and put it up in a bun. I looked in the mirror and smiled at myself. "You did it, you got rid of the asshole". I made myself a coffee and a bagel with cream cheese and went out on my deck. I loved it out there. It was peaceful and quiet. I just heard some crickets, birds and an occasional airplane going overhead. I ate my bagel and sipped on my coffee. I looked over at Charlie's and he was outside on the side of his house, spraying his car off. He took good care of his property, house and car. He was always doing something around his house. I just sat there watching him. He was putting trash into his barrel. HIs house must be immaculate inside. I have never been inside but I can imagine it. It was immaculate on the outside. He didn't even have a fucking weed in his grass. I giggled a little when I was thinking it. I took my cup and paper plate into the house and came back with some windex and a paper towel to clean the coffee ring and the crumbs. I saw Charlie looking at me out of the corner of my eye. I said I wasn't ready to date, but I might be for Charlie. He was a nice guy and really good looking. I walked back into the house and closed the slider and locked it. I think I will cook the stuff from my garden today. I was having dinner with

Grams at 4:00 so I had plenty of time. All the veggies were in that box and I had it in the corner of my kitchen on the floor. First I made a squash, tomato, onion and pepper casserole. That used up all the squash and tomatoes. I washed the peppers and dried them off and then I cleaned the seeds out and cut them up in strips. I put the strips in a freezer bag, labeled the bag with todays date and put them in the freezer. Now they were ready for recipes. I made roasted Cherry Tomatoes with garlic and seasonings for Bruchetta. I toasted some Italian bread, brushed with olive oil, salt, pepper and garlic powder. I made some stuffing for the Cubanelle Peppers, which consisted of grated white bread, fresh grated garlic, diced onion, diced black olives, salt, pepper, olive oil, some seasoned bread crumbs and a little water so they barely stuck together. I stuffed the peppers and put them in a frying pan with a little olive oil, covered them and let them steam for a bit and then took the cover off so I could brown them up. You can eat them just like they are for dinner or on the side with a burger, steak or chicken. I let them cool off and put them in the fridge for during the week. The cucumbers I put in my veggie bin, wrapped in saran wrap. I would make a salad with them during the week. I boiled some eggs for egg salad and made some tuna salad for lunch during the week. Sometimes I took leftovers to work and shared with Stephanie. I think I will bring her a few cucumbers and yellow squash tomorrow. I had an over abundance of them. My box was empty. I put the cucumbers and squash in a brown bag for Stephanie and put it near my lunch bag so I wouldn't forget it. I packed some of the veggie casserole in a tupperware and also a couple of stuffed peppers for Grams. I would bring it to her this afternoon.

I changed my clothes and went to pick up Grams for dinner. Tonight we were going to Buddy's Bar-B-Q. We both loved this place and we frequented it a lot. A bunch of nice people worked here and the food was outstanding. They are known for their smoked meats. They had the best chili cheese fries.   We had a nice dinner. I told her about Charlie and how I had him over for coffee. I told her he was super nice and he wasn't pushy and he helped me to pick the veggies in my garden and carried them to the house for me. We talked a little after dinner and she thanked me for taking her out. She told me she didn't want to go to the movies, so I dropped her off and gave her the food I made, and she wished me a good work week.

I didn't need to put in anymore overtime. I only did that to stay out of the house and away from asshole. I told my boss that I would be working regular hours and thanked her for helping me out. I was now working 8:00 to 5:00 with an hour for lunch. If I didn't log out for lunch and skipped it, I was allowed to leave at 4:00. I didn't usually skip it, because I was starving and it was time spent with Stephanie. I gave Steph the veggies I saved for her and she was so happy.

I usually handled about 8 patients per day. We were a pretty busy place. My days were so nice now. I was a normal person working normal hours and I loved it. I actually had time for myself when I got home. I had time to relax on my deck. I had time to make some of my favorite dinners, to take a walk, water my garden and pick the veggies that were ready and putter around my backyard. I haven't been able to do any of these things in a very long time. I loved being single. No one to boss you around and tell you what you can and can't do. If I ever get married again, I will be wearing the pants or at least be even with my next partner. No more bossy assholes for me. I had more than my share of that shit.

Friday afternoon came quick and I was looking forward to the weekend. I cancelled with Steph earlier and told her I didn't feel like partying. She didn't want to either. I got home and I went to water my garden. Charlie's backyard abutted mine so his garden was close to mine. It was 5:30 and I don't think he was home. I didn't see his car in the driveway. I finished watering and found some more tomatoes and I picked some basil for my tomato salad. Some nights I would just make a big tomato salad with red onion, fresh basil, mozzarella, cucumbers, black olives, spices and olive oil and dunk Italian bread into it. This was going to be tonights dinner and I was looking forward to it. Plus, it was quick and easy and very little cleanup. I came inside and washed my hands and put my speakers on and started playing one of my playlists. I liked Bluesy Rock and guitar music. I was addicted to it. I turned it up a bit and it was a little bit loud, but nothing that anyone could hear outside. I made my salad and danced in the kitchen while making it and I was enjoying myself. My doorbell rang and it startled me. I went to the side door and peeked through the curtain. It was Charlie. I opened the door for him and said, "Hi Charlie, Come on in". He said, "Hi, how was your day? I brought you a small watermelon and a spaghetti squash as promised". I asked if he ate yet and he said he just got home. I told him I was just making a loaded tomato salad. "Interested in joining me?". He said, "I don't know what a loaded tomato salad is, but I'm in for trying it." I added some tomatoes and other ingredients so it was big enough for two people. I added more basil and spices and another cucumber and hit it with some more olive oil. "Grab that Italian Bread Charlie and we will go out on the deck to eat. OK?" He gave me such a big smile. "Sure thing. I can't wait to try this Loaded Tomato Salad. I brought out 2 soup bowls, 2 forks, a bunch of napkins and he grabbed the big bowl without me asking. I asked him if he wanted to try my stuffed cubanelle peppers and he said yes, so I warmed up a couple and brought them out. We went out to the deck and he helped me set it up. I sat with my back facing the tall trees and he sat facing me. He tasted the cubanelles and loved them. I told him I would write the recipe down and he told me he would rather have me make them for him and laughed. I laughed and agreed that I would do that. I told him to dunk the Italian bread into the oil while eating the tomatoes. He took a forkful and dunked his bread and raised his eyebrows. "Wow, that's fucking delicious. I mean it. The flavor just bursts in your mouth. This is outstanding." I smiled at him and said, "Yup. I love eating this for supper in the summer. It's quick and easy and delicious.". He asked me what I put in it and I told him its basically everything from the garden and just add the kitchen sink and he started laughing. "There are no specific measurements or anything. Just what you see and it's a good way to use the fruits of your garden". He told me he didn't have any basil. I told him that I had enough for the whole neighborhood and he could pick as much as he needed. "It roots well too. You can cut some and root it in a glass on your kitchen windowsill and then just plant it. You don't need to ask me, just take what you need". We talked for a while. He was very sociable. He asked me what I did for a living and I told him I was a full-time nurse at Holston Valley Medical Center. He said, "That is impressive Meggie". I asked him what he did and he told me he was an FBI agent in Oak Ridge. I must have looked shocked. He said, "What?". I said, "Wow, I never knew that. Is your job dangerous?". He said, "Sometimes, it depends on what job I am doing. Most of the time, I am at my desk". I told him I was also impressed. "Do you carry a gun Charlie?" He said he carried when he was at work only. I said, "Oh, I see". I sat back in my chair. He said, "Oh, don't be afraid of me because of that Megs". I told him I wasn't afraid of him at all but just wanted to know. He chuckled and sat back in his chair. He whispered across the table, "Looks like we have some nosey neighbors. Someone is peeking through the bushes." He was laughing. "I loved this loaded tomato salad and I think I will try making this. Thank you so much for inviting me. So I have a question for you." I said, "Go for it". He said, "Um, do you wanna go to dinner with me tomorrow night? I know you said you weren't ready to date, but I would love to take you out." I looked at him and hesitated a bit. "Um. I like you Charlie, I really do. I would love to go to dinner with you, but not sure I want to get involved so soon". He shook his head and said, "Is that a yes?". I laughed a nervous laugh and said, "Yes, it is a yes". He smiled, "Ok, we can take it real slow. That is fine with me". I looked at him and said, "Ok, I have a question for you". He said, "Go for it" and he laughed. "Have you ever been married or been engaged? And how many girlfriends have you had?" He smiled at me and said, "That is 3 questions my lady, but I will answer all of them and you owe me 2". I laughed at him. "Ah ha, so, you are a comedian now?" He said, "So, I have never been married or engaged and I have had 4 girlfriends from high school till now and, seeing as I know what your next question will be, I will tell you that none of them worked out because they were either too bossy, they wanted to take over my house, they were more interested in money or they cheated on me." I felt bad now and said, "Oh Jeez, I am sorry I asked. Sounds like you gave a reason for each one." He said, "Oh don't feel bad, those *were* the reasons for each of them. I am looking for a partner in crime, if you will. Someone to love and to love me back, to share my life with and my dreams with. Someone to confide in, to have dinner with and someone who will be there for me and me with them. I don't think that is asking to much, do you? Tell me the truth." I looked at him and said, "Wow, that is a lot!. NO JUST KIDDING, REALLY. I love what you are looking for. It's a fair ask and that is what I need in my life. I just don't want someone to tell me what I can and can not do, run my life and give me shit. I think I want the same things you do, plus I would like to have a couple of kids and have a family." He said, "Oh yeah, I forgot that part. I would love to have a couple kids of my own. It sounds like we want the same things in life, but let's take it slow. I don't wanna force you into dating me or anything like that. Let's just have dinner and see how it goes". I agreed with him. He stayed for a little while and helped me clean up. It wasn't much, but he rinsed the dishes for me and put them in the dishwasher and I went out to clean up the table on the deck. When I came back, everything was done. I said, "I might have to keep you around, seeing as you do dishes". He laughed and said, "I appreciate that you had me for supper and it was really good. Thank you so much". I said, "Well, I am glad you enjoyed it and I was happy to have you. I enjoy your company". He said, "That's what I'm talking about. Good Food and Company. How is 4:00 tomorrow? I would like to take you to the Terrace View Restaurant. Does that sound ok to you?" I told him it sounded wonderful and that I take my Gramma out all the time. "Oh you have a Gramma. That is so nice of you to take her out to dinner. You are lucky Megs". I told him to come outside to the deck because I wanted to tell him a story. "If you can and you have time, I would like to tell you something". He started walking to the deck. "Sure, I have all the time in the world". I grabbed a couple beers and asked him if he was interested and he said yes. I opened them up and brought them out to the deck. I sat and told him my story of how my parents had died in a car accident and that my Gramma took care of me since I was 12 and that I treasured her and I take her out once a week to go eat dinner. Sometimes its during the week and sometimes the weekend, but I always did it, no matter what. He looked at me and said, "You are a sweet person Megs and don't let anyone tell you different. I think that is the greatest thing that you both still get together and that you take her to dinner. I love that". I told him that no matter what, I would do this till the day she died. "She gave me everything I ever needed. She is my mom, my dad and my gramma all rolled into one. I just need you to know this because it was a problem with 'asshole'. He raised his eyebrows. "Jeez, how could that be a problem? Why because you weren't there waiting on him hand and foot?" I said, "Exactly". He said, "Well you won't have that problem with me. I will even join you if it's something you would like, unless you like the time to yourself with her. It's up to you". I smiled at him. "Well, I will leave that up to Grams. Maybe you could meet her on Sunday? I think that is the day I will take her out. Do you want to come with us?" He smiled at me and said, "I would love to meet Grams and it would be my pleasure to take you both out to dinner. I know a great place". I said, "You don't have to pay for us, but I would like you to meet her." He insisted on taking us both out. I didn't want to argue about who was paying, so I just said, "Ok, Thank you." We hung out on the deck till about 9:00 and then he went home. He gave me a peck on the cheek and thanked me for my company and dinner.

I woke up on Saturday morning and just laid in bed for a while. I was feeling so happy. The sun was shining in through my blinds and it felt good on my skin. I stretched my arms and legs and made some stretching noises and then got up to use the bathroom and brush my teeth. I threw on my silk robe and tied it in a knot around my waist. I used my coffee pot instead of the Keurig and made a whole pot of coffee for myself. I intended on drinking at least half of it, on the deck, in the sunshine. I brought my kindle out to the deck to read some more of a book that I picked out. Lately, I enjoyed reading romance stories. I never really read books before, except in school, when I had to. But I found an author that I really enjoyed. I brought the pot of coffee out, along with the sugar and creamer and my cup and spoon. I settled in to read and sip coffee. I looked out back and saw Charlie watering his garden. "Hey Megs, Good Morning". I nodded and said, "Good Morning Charlie. I have a pot of coffee over here if you are interested". He said, "Thanks Megs, but I have a few things to take care of and then some grocery shopping, but I appreciate the invite. See ya later". I waved at him. I ended up drinking half of that pot all by myself and I had such a nice morning out there. I finished my book on the kindle. I headed inside to shower and get dressed. I put my cup in the sink and poured the leftover coffee into a jar and put it in the fridge, along with the creamer for ice coffee another day. I put on a blue sundress with some cute sandals and put my hair up in a comb. It was long so it was up, but a lot of it was hanging down to my shoulders and it looked cute. I think I will make a dessert for later. Maybe Grams would like some. I usually give her half of my desserts that I make. I looked in my pantry for a box mix of some kind. I really wasn't sure what to make, but I didn't want to spend a lot of time doing it. I found a cinnamon streusel mix and I made that. It was quick and easy. I made it into a coffee cake. I cut a piece and ate it for breakfast. I cooled it and covered it and put it in the microwave. I was thinking about dinner tonight with Charlie and wondering if I was going into this too fast. Should I just be by myself for a while and enjoy being me? I knew Charlie meant business. He wanted me and I knew it. He told me he was 32 and that he wanted a family. He might have said he would go slow, but will he at his age? It's partly my fault too, because every time I see him, I invite him over. I like him that's why. I think it's all my fault. I really do invite him over every single time, so I am egging him on. If I egg him on, then I have to put up with the circumstances. I guess there is nothing wrong with dating and having some fun. He IS a nice guy and we both want the same things in life. I guess I will just go with the flow. I want him too.

I grabbed my dust cloth and the pledge and headed to my bedroom. I made the bed and dusted the furniture in the whole house, then got out my vacuum and then I washed all the floors and cleaned the bathroom. I checked my fridge for old food and threw a couple things away. I started the dishwasher and wiped my counters down. There…Everything was done. It took about 1 1/2 hours to clean, but now it was done and I didn't want to do it on Sunday. I set my house alarm and went to the grocery store for a few things. I needed more creamer for coffee, I bought hamburger meat, a package of hotdogs and some buns. I got some lunchmeat at the deli and got some sandwich rolls, lettuce, some ice cream, a brownie mix and I picked up a can of tuna and elbows to make some macaroni salad. That's all I needed. I took it home and brought my groceries in. I put in my new code for the alarm 3-0-3-2. I changed the code after asshole left. I locked my door and then put my groceries away. I got busy and made some macaroni salad for during the week and washed the bowls so they wouldn't take up a lot of room in my dishwasher. I emptied my dishwasher and got that done. I separated the hotdogs, 2 to a package and froze them and made some hamburgers and put those in the freezer. I folded up all my grocery bags and put them in the closet. Now I had to figure out what I was going to wear to dinner and I still had to call Grams and see if she wanted to go to dinner tomorrow and meet Charlie.

"Hi Grams. How's everything?". She told me she was fine. I asked her if she wanted to go out tomorrow and she said yes. "Do you want to meet Charlie Grams? He would like to take us both out for dinner or would you prefer to keep it just me and you?" She said, "I would love to meet Charlie and I think it's nice that he wants to come with you and meet me and that he is paying for dinner. He sounds like a winner to me". I told her we were taking it slow and not rushing into anything and that he was taking me out to dinner tonight. She told me she was happy for me. "See you tomorrow about 4:00 p.m. ok Grams? I think we are going to the Smokehouse Bar n Grill." She said, "Sounds good to me".

I went to my closet to look for a nice dressy dress. I wanted to look really nice. I wanted to look elegant. There is nothing that says elegant like a slim plain black dress dressed up with jewelry. I wore my hair down but pinned it back away from my face with silver pins. I wore a silver necklace with a heart on it and my dangling heart earrings. I had a silver slinky belt to go around my waist and I wore black heels. I looked in the mirror and said out loud, "Girl you look good" and I walked into the kitchen. It was 3:30. I took a couple swigs out of a bottle of water. I went into the bedroom and opened my closet to find my little black clutch. I put my keys, wallet, kleenex, lipstick, perfume, breath mints, a hair tie and my tiny hand sanitizer in it. I was ready to go. I was actually excited to go out with Charlie. The only time I went out now was with my Gramma. Sorry Grams, but you are not a man and I need this.

Charlie was right on time. He knocked at the side door and I peeked through the curtain at him. I opened the door and he stepped in. "Holy Shit Megs, you look, you look fucking gorgeous. Wow. You are a beauty". I thanked him blushing slightly. I said, "You look really nice Charlie. And very handsome too". He was wearing black dress pants and a light blue dress shirt and he had on black boots. He had a cross around his neck and he had a ring on his right middle finger. Wow, he looked so nice all dressed up. He walked me to the car and opened my door. His jacket was in the car, on a hanger in the backseat. I asked him, "Charlie, where is this place you are taking me too?" He said, "Oh, you haven't been there? It's called Terrace View Marina and Restaurant and it's in Spring City. It's about 27 miles from here. It's on Watts Bar Lake." We had some good conversation on the way. I told him that my Gramma wanted to meet him and she said she would love to go out to dinner tomorrow. He was happy with that.

We got there and it was a little crowded but we didn't have to wait for a table. He pulled my chair out for me and I sat and he pushed me in. The waitress came to the table and welcomed us. She handed us menus and took our drink order. I ordered a margarita. They were my favorite. Charlie ordered a beer. He told me he wasn't much of a drinker and usually just drank a beer or two. That was more than fine with me. I told him that I usually had one or two margaritas and that was it for me. He told me that whatever I ordered was good. He comes here a lot and said everything was excellent. I ordered the Catfish Dinner. It consisted of Crispy catfish tenders and it came with homemade Cole slaw, grits and hushpuppies. Charlie ordered The Colonel's Basket, which had a mix of fried shrimp and catfish with the Cole slaw, grits and hush puppies. He ordered the BBQ Nachos as an appetizer. It was smoked pulled pork that was smothered in BBQ sauce and sprinkled with shredded cheese, black beans, corn, jalapeños, sour cream and fresh chives. OMG it was to die for. So friggin good.   And the Catfish was outrageously delicious. He was right. Everything was delicious. We had such a good time and we did a lot of talking and there were a lot of questions and answers and we were really getting to know each other. He lived behind me for years and all I knew about him was that his name was Charlie. He walked me around the outside of the restaurant to show me the lake. It was so pretty at night with all the lights on around the edges of the lake. We turned our backs to the lights and he took a selfie of us both with the lights behind us. It was such a cool picture. We really got along very well and liked the same things. Charlie has a sister that lives in California. She is 4 years older than him and her name is Angela. She is married with 4 children. He said he went to visit her last summer. She has a big beautiful house and her husband is rich, so she doesn't need to work. He looked at me and said, "I am not rich Megs, but I can give you a happy life". I leaned into his shoulder. "I am not looking for a rich guy Charlie, I am looking for someone that I can love and that will love me back. I am looking for someone that will protect me and keep me safe. I am looking for someone that can give me a family and that will make me happy." He put his head down and we met for a kiss. He turned me towards him and kissed me with an open mouth. God he was so hot. I never had this with asshole. I never felt this before. There was electricity shooting down my neck and into my body and it went down to my toes. I wanted more of this. He kissed me again and it was like the skies opened up and I was being struck by lightening. Holy Shit. Ok, I found my guy. He was it and he was right in my own backyard. He pulled me into him and hugged me and kissed me over and over. His hugs were tight and made me feel secure and safe. He had a very muscular build with large arms and I could feel how strong he was. He had a mustache and a small strip of beard from under his mouth but just in the center that went straight to his chin. I don't know why, but it turned me on. I just had to look at it and I was turned on. I never really noticed it until tonight with the kiss.

4

HOUSE ALARM

We walked back to the car, hand in hand and he opened my door. He got in the car, kissed me again and then we started for home. I wanted to know more about his job. "So, Charlie, at your job, do you have to wear a badge?". He told me when he was out of the office he had one in his pocket. "Does it have a number or letters on it that identify you?" He said, "Yes, my badge number is 3032." I looked at him shocked. "Are you fucking kidding me right now?". We weren't on the road yet, we were still in the parking lot. He stopped the car and said, "What's wrong Meg?". I said, "Charlie, you aren't gonna believe me, but I changed my alarm code after asshole left and I changed it to 3-0-3-2." He stared at me and then smiled. "Well, then, I was meant to be right?" I told him numbers meant something to me and I did think it was a sign. "Like, I am 30 and you are 32. There it is again". He just stared at me. "Wow, you might be on to something". And he chuckled. I didn't think he believed in that stuff, but he made me believe he did tonight. He drove me home and walked me to the door. "Lock up tight ok? Put your alarm back on and I will see you tomorrow". I said, "Charlie, Thank you so much for dinner. I really enjoyed it with you". He took a step inside my door and gave me that kiss. "Will you date me now?" I looked at him lovingly. "I guess I have to now.

I mean after all those kisses, those kisses". He kissed me again and said, "Yeah, I felt it too". He walked out the door with the biggest smile on his face. I locked up and put my alarm back on 3032 and smiled to myself. Was this really a sign that he was meant to be with me? Am I just being dumb believing in this number stuff? We shall see. We shall see. I undressed and hung my dress up and kicked off my heels into my closet and then straightened them out on the shelf. I dumped my clutch into my purse and put it back in my closet. I took off all my jewelry and put it back into my jewelry box, slipped on my nightgown and went to brush my teeth. I went to the kitchen for a bottle of water, shut off all the lights and went to bed and I had a big smile on my face. I thought to myself. 'I think I found him, I really think I found him'.

I woke up Sunday morning and it was raining hard and it was hitting my bedroom window. I looked at the clock and it was only 6:30 a.m. I went back to sleep and woke up around 8:45 a.m. The rain had stopped and the sun was peeking through the clouds and the birds were singing. Well, one thing for sure, I don't have to water my garden today. I got up and used the bathroom, put my robe on and went to the kitchen to make myself a coffee. I blew a whisp of hair out of my face and checked my face out in the toaster. Eww. I looked like hell. I didn't take off my makeup and it was smudged all over my face. My hair looked like I got in a fight with my pillow. I went back to the bathroom and washed my face off and brushed my hair out. That's better. How did I not see this when I was brushing my teeth? I don't think I even looked in the mirror.

I sat in my living room to have my coffee because my deck was all wet. I put my speakers on and put my playlist on. I had the TV on, but my sound was off. I despised commercials and it seemed like that was all there was. There were more commercials than actual TV shows or even weather. 20 minutes of commercials and 10 minutes of weather. I hardly ever watched TV unless it was Netflix because there were no commercials. I started dreaming of last nights date with Charlie. It was an actual date and he knew it when he asked me out. He was just trying to make me feel like it was a friendly dinner. It was until the kisses happened, at least for me. No, I am lying. I felt like I was on a date with him and I knew it wasn't friendly. I knew it and when we went outside, I was waiting for him to kiss me. There, I said it. I really have feelings for him already and that's why when I see him outside, I talk to him and invite him over. That's why I made a whole pot of coffee yesterday. I was hoping he would come over and help me drink it. I like him a lot, a whole lot. And I don't want to be friends anymore.

I had nothing really to do today and we weren't going out to dinner for another 7 hours. I got up and went to take a quick shower and get dressed. I just put my sweats on for now. I loved doing nothing in sweats. I made my bed and opened the curtains in the bedroom and living room. I made myself another cup of coffee and some scrambled eggs, breakfast sausage and a piece of toast and sat in the kitchen to eat it. I cleaned up my mess. I decided to put my hair up for now, I kept having to blow it out of my face. It was fly away today. I will probably wear it up tonight and put some hairspray in it to keep it in place. It was just casual tonight. He was taking us to the Smokehouse Bar and Grill. Grams and I usually went to Buddy's, so this will be a little different for the both of us.

I cut my cinnamon streusel in half and put the other half in a container for Grams. I took a piece and ate it. I was full, but I couldn't resist it. I was just taking my last bite and my house alarm went off. It was so fucking loud and it scared the crap out of me. I started walking around the house to see what was going on. I wasn't turning it off until I knew. My phone rang and it was the security company. I told them I was walking around. They said they would send the police to check it out and to leave the alarm on. All of a sudden there was a banging on my side door. "MEGS, OPEN UP, ITS CHARLIE, MEGS ARE YOU OK? OPEN UP ITS CHARLIE". I ran and opened the door. He grabbed me and hugged me and pecked me on the forehead. He asked me what was going on and I told him the cops were coming and that I didn't see anything but I didn't go upstairs yet. He had his gun on him. The cops were at my door and Charlie put his gun in the back of his pants. He let them in and told them that we hadn't checked upstairs yet. He was following them upstairs and told me to stay put. I heard him telling them that he was FBI and he had a gun on him. They asked to see his badge and they were talking. Well, they found out the reason for the alarm going off. It seems Bill had climbed up the side of the house from the tree and broke a window and the alarm went off. He was hiding under the bed in the spare room. What a dumb fuck! Did he think no one would find him under there? He had another bag of cocaine in his hands. Where the hell did he get this from? He started telling the cops that I was hiding it for him. I looked at Charlie horrified and I was shaking my head NO, NO. The cops were looking around my house upstairs and came across a loose floor board with a rug over it. I told him that the board was raised and I kept stubbing my toe on it, so I put the small rug over it. The cop pushed down on the loose board and it opened up and inside there was a bunch of cocaine in bags and a gun underneath it. I was horrified. "OMG, How could you do this to me? You fucking asshole". One of the cops that came was one of the ones that came when he had thrown the bottle at me. He looked at me and said, "I have to take you down to the station. I know it wasn't you and you had no idea it was there, but I have to". Charlie shook his head and said I had to go to clear my name and he would come with me. I broke down crying and that bastard started laughing at me. He said, "I told you I would get back at you". That was all the cop had to hear and he had his body cam going. The cop laughed at him and said, "You just cleared her. I have all this on my body cam". They dragged him out of the house with his handcuffs on. They confiscated the cocaine and took the gun out of the floor with gloves on. The cop looked at Charlie and said, "You might want to put a nail in this board for this young lady". Charlie smiled at him and thanked him and then he grabbed me for a really tight hug. I was still sniffling. I couldn't believe that this just happened to me. "Why is he out of jail?" Charlie said, "I don't know, but he will definitely be going back for quite a while." I grabbed him closer to me and hugged him. "Thank you for coming over Charlie. I don't know what I would have done without you". He said, "You are ok Meggie". He said he would call someone to get the window fixed. He took me downstairs and the cops left. He was on his phone for about 10-15 minutes, standing out on my deck. He came in and said he had someone coming to repair the window and he would stay until it was done. I was still shaky.   I still couldn't believe this happened. "Where the hell did he get that gun Charlie?" He told me the cops would take care of it. I said, "He could have killed me with that gun." Charlie hugged me and said, "But he didn't and you are going to be ok". He kissed me. He said, "I don't think we should go out to dinner because you are really upset.

5

MEETING GRAMS

Why don't you call Grams and we can pick her up and bring her back here and I will order some dinner in. Is that ok?" I told him that would be fine and I really didn't feel like going out. I called my Gramma and told her what just happened and said that we would come and get her as soon as my window got fixed. She agreed that we shouldn't go out. "We can skip this week Meegs. We don't have to go out". I told her we were not skipping and that we would pick her up once my window was fixed. She laughed and said, "Ok, Meegs". I had her on speaker phone. Charlie said, "She calls you Meegs?" I shook my head yes and said, "She has called me that since day one and she is the only one". He told me that we would still have Smokehouse Bar & Grill, but he would have it delivered. "Do you have a printer? I can print out the menu so you and Grams can look at it, ok?" I told him I had a printer in my spare room on the desk with my laptop. He asked for my password so he could hook up to my internet and told me to stay here. "I don't want you upset at the crime scene." And he chuckled. He printed it and came downstairs. "Megs, do you have any other loose floor boards that you know of?" I told him I wasn't aware of any. He told me that he would check the whole house for me at another time just to make sure. "If you find one, don't touch it, I will take care of it, ok?" I shook my head. He said, "That guy is a piece of work. I wonder how long he had that in the floor?" I told him, "I don't know, but I hope there are no more loose floor boards and that he didn't hide anything anywhere else in my house. That's where he got the bag that he was trying to hide under the mattress".

He handed me the menu and said, "Sit and relax and take a look at the menu and take your mind off of this". The doorbell rang and he went to get it. It was the guy to fix the window. He knew him, because they shook hands and the guy said, "How the hell have you been?" They both went upstairs and I heard Charlie telling him what happened. He came down and he had my bedroom window with him. He said he would be back in an hour and that he closed the bedroom door so no bugs would come down. As promised, he came back in an hour and he had a brand new piece of glass in the window. He was up there with Charlie for about an hour. They had to put it back in and put all the wood back around it. When he came back, he told me that it would need to be repainted but it was good and solid. I got my checkbook and he was shaking his hand at me. "Nope it's all good". I was shaking my head, no. "No, no, it's not, please let me pay you". He said, "No, Charlie took care of this, so your argument is with him. I am good". I looked at Charlie and he was fooling around. He was heading for the door and said, "Well, I gotta get going". I yelled. "Charlie, get your ass back here" and the window guy laughed and said, "Good Luck, Dude" Charlie came up to me when the guy left and said, "Please let me do this for you. I wanted to or I wouldn't have. I hate fighting about money ok?" I thanked him and gave him a kiss and said ok. I said, "I just want you to know that I really appreciate you being here with me during all this and you don't have to pay for my repairs, but I also appreciate it". He looked at me and said, "I know you are into the number thing, so I guess you will want to know this. The total for the window was $303.20. I am only telling you this because you think that number means something, not because I want you to pay me back. I am beginning to believe you". I just looked at him with my mouth open. "OMG. That is unbelievable." It was 3:00 p.m. so I called my Gramma and told her we were coming to get her. She said, "I'm ready Meegs". Charlie drove me to her house and I introduced him to her. I saw it in her eyes. She was smitten with him. I got her buckled into the back seat and we took off. She talked to Charlie the whole way back to my house. She was asking him all kinds of questions and the last one was "What do you do for a living Charles?" He said, "Don't get scared Grams, but I am an FBI agent". She looked at him and said, "Why would I be scared. At least I know Meegs will be protected and so will I". She was flirting with him. He told her to call him Charlie and she said, "Why can't I call you Charles?" He said, "Well, you can, but I am more comfortable with Charlie". She agreed that she would call him Charlie. We got back to the house and Charlie took her by the arm to help her out of the back seat. She was looking up at him and smiling. My grams loved him and that made me happy. I never saw her smile like that when I was with Bill. She always grimaced at him. We got into the house and he told her to sit at the dining room table because there was a menu for her to look at. Then he said, "You know what, let's get a Smorgasbord of food tonight. And then we can all pick at whatever we want. How does that sound?". I couldn't get a word in edgewise. She said, "Oh that sounds wonderful Charlie". I just smiled and shook my head yes. He smiled at me. "Is there anything special you would like Grams?" And she said, "Nope, you just order anything you want". He ordered a basket of beer battered onion rings and French Fries, some mozzarella sticks and some fried pickles. A French Dip sandwich and told them to slice it, a Philly cheesesteak and slice it, a pulled pork sandwich, sliced, a buffalo Chicken Wrap, a smokehouse Quesadilla, a half rack of ribs, a side of Cole slaw, Mac and cheese, whipped red potatoes, baked beans and a loaded baked potato. When they delivered it, it took up almost the whole dining room table. We cut everything up in pieces so we could try everything. There was so much fucking food, we could all eat it for the rest of the week. I sent Grams home with some, Charlie took some and I kept the rest. We stuffed our faces and I gave Charlie a beer and me and Grams had coke. The food was outstanding and I would definitely love to go there. Grams had such a good time with Charlie. Charlie loved her too. I made a pot of decaf coffee and we had that cinnamon streusel for dessert. I gave Grams her half to take home. She loved dessert. Charlie and I took her home around 9:00. He walked her into her house and made sure her doors were locked. She kissed him on the cheek and thanked him for a wonderful night of food and conversation. As we were driving back, Charlie said, "Your

Grams is a wonderful person, Megs. She is feisty and I think she has a crush on me". I laughed and told him that I thought so. I told him that she wouldn't let me get a word in all night. He said he noticed that too. I told him that I let her because she is alone most of the time and she had a good time tonight. He said, "I can see why you love her so much. She has a great personality and she is smart as a whip." I told him I would never miss a week, ever. "If something ever happened to her and I missed a week, I wouldn't be able to live with myself". He said, "I hear ya".

6

DINNER DATES AND NOSEY NEIGHBORS

He dropped me off and walked me to the door. "Do you want me to help you clean up in there?". I told him he didn't have to. "You probably spent a couple hundred dollars on all that food, you don't need to clean it up too". He stepped inside my door and said, "I insist" and he pushed my door open all the way. I smiled at him. "Oh yeah, you have your containers of food here too". He bent over and kissed me and I felt it down to my toes. "We are dating now right?". I said, "We are, yes, we are". He wiped the dining room table down and I put my food in containers and put them in the fridge. I had one ready for tomorrow's lunch. "We are gonna be eating this food all week. It was so good and thank you again". He came up behind me and said, "You are not getting rid of me that quick. It's only 9:30. He put my alarm on and he turned me around and picked me up off the ground and put me over his shoulder and carried me upstairs. I was laughing and giggling. "What are you doing sir?". He was laughing too and said, "I am taking you upstairs. What does it look like?" He plopped me on the bed and he laid down next to me and put the TV on and he grabbed me and put his arm around me and he held me while we watched TV. I had my head on his chest and he kept kissing me on my head and my forehead while we watched TV. He stayed until 11:00 and then said he had to get going. He gave me a long kiss before we went downstairs. He made me lock up and set the alarm again. "See you tomorrow Megs". I said, "Thank you for everything today Charlie". I handed him his food containers and he blew me a kiss and left.

Monday comes too soon, but I had a good weekend, minus the break-in from asshole. I got my nurse's uniform on and put my hair up in a bun, took my lunch out and put it in my tote bag. I would eat leftovers for supper so I didn't need to take anything out of the freezer. I would eat some bbq stuff and have some macaroni salad with it. I should have given some to Charlie. I can't eat all this. Well, I can ask him later if he wants some. I saw Stephanie at lunch and filled her in on what happened and also my new love life. She was horrified over the break-in and my boss heard too. "You just can't get rid of that jerk can you?". I shook my head. "He is a pain in my fucking ass. And Charlie ended up paying to have my window repaired." My day went by fast and I couldn't wait to get home. I changed out of my uniform and went out to water my garden first.   I had some veggies ready and I balanced them in my arms and carried them to the house and then turned off my hose. I shook my cushions out and stood them up to drain any leftover water out of them, but they were actually dry. Ahh, this was good because now I could eat out here tonight. I miss eating on my deck. I wasn't hungry yet, so I went in the garage and got my little lawnmower and went over the lawn in the backyard quick. I looked up and Charlie was standing there with his trimmer and he was going all along the bushes, all around the garden and the fence on the other side my property. His lawn was already done. He finished and I told him to come up and get something to drink and I put my lawnmower back in the garage. I didn't see him anywhere. Where did he go? He went home and was coming back with his food containers from yesterday. He was smiling. "I brought my dinner. I thought we could eat together. Is that ok?". I smiled back at him and said, "I was going to ask you, because I have some macaroni salad that I made on Saturday that we need to eat". He went in my fridge and got it out and grabbed a bottle of water and downed it. He was sweating. I threw a hand towel at him. He wiped himself down. "Ah that's better". I thanked him for trimming. "You saved me a job". I turned my air conditioner down one degree so it would go on. "Do you wanna eat inside Charlie? It's a little warm out there and you are sweating already". He said, "No, I will be ok. There is actually a breeze out there and when you are sitting, you don't sweat". I was glad he said that because I really wanted to eat outside. I think he knew that. He brought the macaroni salad out. I brought some paper plates and napkins and forks. He was heating up his food and then I heated mine up and we both took it outside to eat. He sat down and then he stood up and said, "OH, I forgot something". He came over to me and kissed me and then went to sit back down. I smiled at him. He said, "I missed you today. You are all I thought about". I told him that I missed him too. "I can't concentrate on my work anymore". He laughed at me. I asked him, "You want a beer, soda or water?". He said, "Water if you don't mind".

I got up and got 2 waters and came back to the table. He said, "This macaroni salad is better than the one we got from the restaurant Megs". I blushed. "Aww. Thanks Charlie". He said, "I like eating with you. Better than eating alone". I told him I enjoyed his company too. We cleaned up and he kissed me again and said, "Same time, same place tomorrow? Unless you have other plans". I looked at him and said, "Same time, Same place tomorrow, no plans". He said, "You know what? How bout tomorrow, you come to my house. I want you to see my house." My face must have lit up. I was waiting for this invitation. "Ok. Yes, that sounds great. I would love that". He laughed and said, "Can you bring the macaroni salad?" I told him I would and chuckled at him.

He was so easy going, charming, compassionate and warmhearted and he made you want to be like him. I trusted him and usually that took me a long time to do with people. We went upstairs to watch TV again and there was more kissing than last night. And it wasn't my forehead and head tonight. It was getting very intense. He was such a romantic guy. He left again around 11:00 p.m. It was an awesome few hours.

Another day at work and I was able to concentrate a little today, but I couldn't wait to finish up for the day. Finally, I was done and I headed home. I changed out of my uniform and put on a pair of shorts and a sleeveless blouse and my flip flops. It was a lot warmer today than yesterday. Yesterday it was 88 and today it was 95. I took out the macaroni salad and loaded up a container with it and then took out the stuffed peppers and packed those into another container. Then I took out a container of leftover food from Sunday night. I put all this in a shopping bag with handles and put the rest of the stuff back in the fridge. I was excited to go over his house. I looked out back and he wasn't home yet. I got a glass and put some ice in it and poured myself a zero coke and went out on the deck. I put the overhead fan on to cool it down a bit. I think tomorrow, if it's cooler, I will mow my front yard. It only takes about 15 minutes and it was looking a bit ragged. I didn't want to be the only person on my street that didn't take care of my lawn. I never did the front and back on the same day. I don't know why, I just never did. Maybe because of the heat. My backyard was very big and it usually took me over a half hour to do. I had a small lawnmower, so I could handle it myself, because, you know, asshole never did it. So it took me longer to mow. I managed to do it every other week and keep it nice. Tomorrow on my way home, I was going to stop at the car wash and get my car clean and park it in the garage so it wouldn't get dirty with the grass. My garage was actually a 2 car garage, but I had my lawnmower and trimmer and a few other things in there. But now that asshole's stuff was out, I had a lot of room in there. I had a closet out there that I kept my gardening stuff in, along with potting soil and steel rods for holding up my plants and planting tape. Stuff like that. I had pots for flowers and seeds and things. I kept it neat and now that asshole's stuff was gone, I needed to reorganize it and get it neat again. I had my rakes, shovels and brooms and I wanted to get something to hang them on so they wouldn't be on the floor of the garage. Maybe Charlie could help me with that. I will ask him tonight. I saw him pulling in from work. He got out of his car and waved to me and went inside. It was still early to be eating dinner, so I just sat there enjoying my soda. I played some music on my phone. I decided to go out front and get my mail because I forgot to pick it up on my way in today. I walked out front to my mailbox and I heard my neighbor across the street. "You didn't wait too long before finding another one did ya?" I turned around to look at her and said, "Excuse me?" She said, "You heard me". I said, "Why don't you mind your own fucking business and get your own life" and walked back to my front door. What a fucking bitch! I hate the people here, I really do. They have nothing better to do than to spy on people. It was probably her peeking through the bushes the other night. I went through my mail and threw away the junk. One bill. That's the kind of mail I like. I walked back to the deck to get my glass and saw Charlie standing in the backyard. He was waving me to come over. I waved back. I went in to get the bag of food and walked down my backyard and into his backyard and up to his side porch. He was waiting for me. I walked in and he kissed me. His place was immaculate, just like I thought it would be. Not even a crumb on his floor. He took the bag from me and looked inside. "MMM. Macaroni salad". I told him what just happened to me at the mailbox. He just looked at me and said, "Are you kidding me? Some people get their jollies off by making trouble". I told him. "I told her to mind her own fucking business and get her own life". He hugged me and told me not to get upset over it. I told him I wasn't but I can't believe these people are watching me. He said, "They have nothing better to do". I told him that I never worried about this before because I was always working and never had the time, like I do now. He said, "You don't have to worry about it now either. Just ignore them. The more you talk to them, the more they know they are getting to you. I have one over here (and he pointed) that is a nosey body. She probably knows you are here now. She is always looking out her side door through the curtains". He showed me his house. It was the same setup that I had, it was just reversed. He had a lot of nice furniture. Expensive furniture and it was decorated beautifully. I was impressed because he was a man and men usually don't know how to decorate. "Wanna eat on the deck?" He asked me. I said that would be fine. He handed me plates, forks, napkins all piled up and he warmed up my food and his food and carried it out with the bag. We set it up and he went back in and came back 10 minutes later with a margarita and a beer. My face lit up and I said, "OH how NICE, Thank you so much". He said, "I figured I owed you one because we didn't go out on Sunday". I told him he didn't owe me a penny. We sat out and ate our dinner and he was really enjoying my macaroni salad. "Mmm good stuff". I smiled at him and told him I was glad he was enjoying it. "Your house is really nice. I like the way its decorated." He told me that he did not decorate it, his sister did. "Oh?" He said, "I can't decorate for shit so I asked her to do it for me. I sent her pictures of my rooms and my furniture and she told me where to put everything." I started laughing because he was laughing while he told me the story. "We face-timed on her husband's phone, while she decorated. She doesn't have an iPhone. She went room by room with me. It was pretty funny, but it came out nice". I told him it was perfect.

We had a really nice dinner together and we hung out until around 9:30 that night. He was so social, but laid back. He was comfortable to be around and I was able to just be myself around him. I even burped in front of him. It was an accident of course, but he didn't even flinch. He just said, "God Bless you". I laughed and he did too. But about 5 minutes later, he burped and I said, "God Bless You" and we both laughed.

7

IS IT LOVE?

The next morning, I went to work and saw Steph and I just had to tell her what was happening. "Steph you have no idea. He is so nice. He is caring and attentive to me." She raised her eyebrows and said, "Have you, you know?" I told her that we haven't. "Not yet, but it's coming Steph. When he kisses me, I feel it down to my toes." She laughed and said, "Yup, it's coming". She patted me on the back and we went back to our jobs. I couldn't wait to get home and see Charlie. I was addicted to him. I loved his company, I loved his voice, I loved how he touched me, I loved how he stroked my hair out of my face, I loved how he was so comfortable around me, I loved his kisses, I loved how he confided in me with everything and I think I actually loved him.

I stopped on the way home to get my car washed. I got home, changed, grabbed a bottle of water out of the fridge and went to water my garden and gather more vegetables. Shit, I forgot to get my mail on the way in. That means I have to walk out front to get it and that means Ms. Nosey across the street will have something else to say to me. Charlie said to just ignore her like she isn't there, so that is what I will do. I walked out my garage, because it was open and grabbed my mail. There she was, on her front porch, watching everyone on the street. She really had no life. I bet she sat there all day. Her eyes were on me, but I never looked at her. I put my mail in the house and then went back to the garage to get my lawnmower out and do the front yard. All of a sudden, Charlie was in my driveway and he came up to me and kissed me and it wasn't just a short kiss. He held me tight and pulled me close to him. Then he whispered in my ear. "Is that her?" I whispered back, "Yup, that's Ms. Nosey". He laughed and said, "Let's give her something to look at". He started kissing me deep and caressing my back and I was caressing his back and then he pulled me into the garage and we went in a dark corner. She got up off the porch to get a better look and started coming across the street. I couldn't believe it. He said, "Watch this". When she got to the edge of my driveway, he came out of the garage running at her. "WHAT THE FUCK ARE YOU DOING? WHAT DO YOU WANT?". She got scared and ran back to her house and went inside. The neighbor on the right side of me saw him and said, "She deserved that". Charlie just smiled at her. I came out of the garage with the lawnmower and started mowing and he got my trimmer out and did the trimming. He kept looking across the street to see if she was peeking out a window, but she wasn't. I said, "Charlie, she probably had a heart attack". He said, "If she did, she deserved it. It's called KARMA". He took the blower out and cleaned all the grass off the driveway and sidewalks and we cleaned up and put everything away. "I see you washed your car today?". I told him I did on the way home. He was sweating and said he was going home to shower quick. I told him I was going to do the same. "Lock your doors before you get in there". He bent over to kiss me. He closed my garage door and we went in through the house and he went out the back door. He turned around half way down my backyard. "Megs? Supper your house?" I told him yes and he smiled and went home. I looked down and he had left a trail of grass from the garage to the slider. I got my vacuum and cleaned it up and then got in the shower quick. I put on a pair of shorts and a sleeveless top and my flip flops and put my hair up and twisted it and pinned it down. I went to the fridge and took out the macaroni salad and the rest of my leftovers. I warmed them all up. This would be the last night I eat them, so I just warmed everything up and Charlie could eat it too. There was a little of everything he ordered. I got paper dishes, forks and napkins and brought it all outside on the deck and set it all up on the table. I started playing my playlist on my phone and left it outside. I had 2 pieces of cinnamon streusel cake left, so I brought that out too. I made 2 ice coffees with extra ice and brought them out. I saw him walking up to my deck. "Hi cutie pie" and he kissed me. "This looks good enough to eat. Is that ice coffee?". I told him it was and it was leftover from the pot I made the other day. He took a sip first thing and said, "Did you ever work for Dunkin' cause this tastes just like it". I told him I got it down to a science and he agreed. As always, we had a good time while having dinner. He looked down and saw grass on the deck. "I dropped some grass out here, I will clean it up". I said, "Don't you even think about it. I will grab the vacuum and clean it later". He said he found grass on his floors too and cleaned it up. "I was full of it. It stuck to me". I didn't say anything about the grass I found because I didn't want him to feel bad. He was big help to me. He did the trimming and blew the grass off the sidewalks and driveway and that was such a big help to me. I told him, "I would still be out there doing it, if it wasn't for you. I appreciate your help. Thank you so much for that." He reached across the table and stroked my hair. "Anything for you Megs". He said, "I have to tell you something, but I don't want you to think I am a creep". I tilted my head and said, "What?". "Please don't think bad of me for this Megs". He looked worried. "I have always liked you and thought you were the most beautiful woman I ever laid eyes on. Anytime I could get a peek at you, I did. I watched you in the garden and mowing your lawn. Not in a bad way, mind you, but I loved you from a distance". I looked at him in disbelief. "You did? You think I am beautiful?" He looked at me and said, "Yes, I think you are and I was sad that you were married to that piece of shit". I told him that I was not upset and I didn't think he was a creep at all and that I was flattered that he was peeking at me. He looked relieved and said, "Phew. Thank God. I wouldn't want anyone telling you something different so I decided to tell you how I felt about you". I told him that I am glad that he did. "You know we have nosey neighbors that have no life whatsoever". He laughed. He said, "Megs, do you have any vacation time? I have a shit load and was wondering if you would like to go on vacation with me". I smiled at him lovingly and said, "I have a shit ton too. Where to?" He looked like I gave him the world on a platter. I can't explain the expression on his face. "Well, I haven't thought about where yet, but we can pick somewhere together? What do you think?" I told him, "I think I need a vacation, no matter where it is. We can figure it out and plan it. It sounds fucking good to me. But I don't have a passport, so it would have to be within the United States". He said he had one and he would help me get one for the future. "There are plenty of places to go here".

We googled places to go on vacation in the United States and we decided to go to Nantucket off the coast of Cape Cod and to visit Cape Cod as well. We decided to go for one week and enjoy everything we could. I was excited because I haven't been on vacation for years. Charlie said, "Don't forget, we will have to take Grams out for dinner before we leave and once we get back". I got out of my chair and hugged him and ended up sitting in his lap. "You make me happy Megs". I told him, "I didn't think I was ready to date Charlie, but its actually overdo. You make me happy too".

So in 1 1/2 weeks, we were leaving for Nantucket. We would fly there and rent a car. He did everything on-line and scheduled our whole trip. We both liked beach and seafood and neither of us have been there. He rented a house, so we had all the amenities. There was even a fire pit out back. The house was close to the beach, so we could walk to it. It only took a few minutes to walk there. I was so excited for this. I didn't want to wait that long. The next week was going to drag. I just knew it would. Isn't that the way it works? When you are looking forward to something, it takes forever to get there.

I took the next day off from work to do a little shopping. I was just so excited.   I needed a couple of new bathing suits, a beach towel, some sundresses, new shorts and tops, sandals and flip flops and other odds and ends. I wanted to look my best for him. Besides, I haven't bought anything new in forever. I deserved this. I am usually out of the house by 7:30 a.m. when I go to work. This gave me time to get a coffee and if I needed to get gas for the car and I wouldn't be late for work. I left to go shopping around 9:30 a.m. At 8:00 a.m. I saw Charlie walking out his side door. He looked at my house and then started walking towards me. He saw me on my deck. "You ok, Megs? Is everything alright?". I told him that I took the day off and I was gonna go shopping for myself. He smiled. "Ok, I thought something was wrong. Have a good time and be careful". He threw me a kiss and he left for work. I finished up my coffee and I was ready to go spend some money on myself. It was way past time to do this. I went to the mall and went into a lot of stores and got a lot cute things. I got things for my hair and I found cute shorts, and leggings and cute blouses and a really pretty evening dress in dark purple. I found a few nice evening dresses and put them in my cart. I found some shoes to go with them and I was so happy with myself. I got some new jewelry, some new sexy underwear and sexy bras. I had someone to wear them for now and I was ready. I bought a couple of tote bags and a small overnight bag to put the small stuff in. I had a suitcase, but needed something smaller. I bought a big purse so I could put stuff in there for traveling only. I bought a new shower puff, liquid shower soap, shampoo and conditioner and a tiny travel hairdryer. I didn't have any of this stuff because I never went anywhere. I took myself out for lunch and then went to Walmart and picked up a few other odds and ends. I stopped at the grocery store and picked up a rotisserie chicken.   I got home around 3:00 p.m. I had such a nice day, all by myself and I had a bunch of new things. I changed my clothes and went to water the garden. There were a lot of veggies ready so I picked them and put them in the grass next to the garden and went up to the house to get my box out of the garage. I opened the door to the garage and I thought I saw something move. UUUUGGGH. It scared me. I backed out and closed the door. I decided to use grocery bags to carry the veggies up. I got them all up to the house and turned the hose off. I got a bottle of water out of the fridge and went out on the deck and put my music on. I plopped in my cushioned chair. I looked at Charlie's house and saw his car in the driveway. Wow. He got home early. I decided to walk over and see him. I knocked at his side door and answered. "Hi Megs. What's up?". I said, "I saw your car and decided to come and say hi. You are home early aren't you?" He said he was home early. He didn't have much to do so his boss sent him home. "Oh that's nice. Am I bothering you?". He said I wasn't, but I felt like I interrupted something. I said, "I can go. I just wanted to invite you to dinner. I picked up a rotisserie chicken". He said, Oh, sounds yummy. I would love to join you. What time?" I said, "I don't know, maybe 5:15 or whenever you are done with what you are doing". He said, "Meg, I am not doing anything and you are not bothering me. I am

glad you came over. Do you want help prepping supper?"
I told him I didn't need any help, but he could come over
whenever he wanted. "Oh Charlie, I almost forgot. I
opened the door to my garage to get my veggie box, and I
saw something moving in there. I got scared, so I closed
the door. Can you check for me?" He said, "Oh jeez, yeah,
let me come over and check on it for you. Let me get my
gun. It might be a snake or a raccoon or something". I told
him if it was a raccoon, I didn't want him to shoot it. He
laughed and said ok.   I left and he said he would be right
over.

I got home and put the rotisserie chicken in the air fryer. I
made some brown gravy and some instant mashed
potatoes and made some broccoli. Charlie came to my
side door, he knocked and came right in. "Mmmm
something smells really good in here". I looked at him, he
bent over to kiss me and I said, "That would be your dinner,
sir". He knew I didn't like guns, so he had it tucked into the
back of his pants. He walked to the garage door and
opened it slowly. He hit the garage door opener on the wall
and the garage opened. He took the shovel I had near the
door and started hitting the cement with it to startle
whatever was in there. All of a sudden, a little animal made
a run for the door. It was a squirrel. Poor thing must have
been in there all night from when we did the grass
yesterday. He came in and told me and said it was all clear
and he shut the garage door. "That happened to me
before, but it was a raccoon."   I thanked him for getting
him out. "Dinner is almost ready. Would you mind getting
the silverware and napkins and drinks out?" He got right

on it. I put butter on the broccoli as it came out of the microwave. I put a serving spoon in it and finished the mashed potatoes and put a serving spoon in that too. I brought those out to the deck. The chicken had two more minutes to go. I took it out and carved it and put a fork on the plate and brought it out. He looked at me and said, "Wow, this is awesome." I asked him to go get the salad and the dressing out of the fridge and he jumped up to get it. He came back with it and had 2 salad bowls too. I smiled at him. He must have been hungry because he dove into that food like he hasn't eaten in a week. He kept saying how nice it was to have a home cooked meal. I told him it was rotisserie chicken that I bought at the store. He still kept saying it was home cooked. He really enjoyed the meal and he kept telling me how much he was loving it. He helped me bring everything back into the house and he went out to clean off the table with windex. I rinsed all the dishes and put them in the dishwasher. He put the leftovers in containers and shoved them in the fridge. "Is this ok like this?" And he pointed to the chicken in a bowl with plastic wrap over it. I told him it was fine and thanked him for helping. I asked him if he wanted a beer and he said he was fine. "I still have water and that's fine. Wanna go back and sit outside?" I said yes, but what I really wanted was to cuddle with him and kiss him. "Yeah, I guess". He started laughing. "Megs, just be yourself. If you wanna stay inside, just say so. I can read you like a book". I looked at him surprised. "What? How did you know I didn't want to go out again?" He laughed at me. He closed the slider and locked it. "You wanna relax down

here and watch TV or upstairs and watch TV.?" I started
going upstairs and he check the door in the kitchen to
make sure it was locked and followed me up.

8

THE CONNECTION

I plopped on the bed and kicked my flip flops off. He took
off his shoes and joined me. It didn't take him long. He
was almost on top of me, kissing me with his hot tongue
and caressing me with his hands, all over. He knew what I
wanted and he wanted it too. He kissed me everywhere
and ripped my clothes off one piece at a time and kissed
what he uncovered. He was hot and panting and that
made me want him more. I pulled at his shirt and he took it
off. I was kissing what I uncovered and he was over
excited and it was showing. We were both undressed,
kissing each other everywhere and it finally happened. We
both laid panting and satisfied and he was staring at me.
He said it. "I love you Megs. I always have, even when I
didn't know you. You knew I wasn't married Meg. You just
used that in your brain to stay away from me, didn't you?"
I smiled at him, but I wouldn't admit that he was right. I
really was attracted to him for the 8 years I lived there and I
never saw a woman with him ever. I knew he wasn't
married and he was right. I kept telling myself he was, so I
would stay faithful to asshole. How the hell did he know
this? He laughed a little and said, "No answer is an
admission". I broke down and told him he was right. "I
have always been attracted to you since I moved here and
then I met asshole, so I told myself you were married. You

are right". He hugged me tight. "I knew it, I knew I was right". I kissed his face all over and he did the same. I felt like I was in high school having my first romance. I really only dated a few guys in high school and only had sex with one, but none of them were ever like this. I never felt like this before. Not even with asshole. I was really in love and I wanted him all the time. I craved having him near me. I needed him and he knew it. I think he needed me too.

He got up and said, "Wanna come with me to the shower?" I got up and went with him. He took my hand when I stepped in. Well, you know what happened in there. I don't think I need to tell you. We got out and dried off and we got dressed. He said, "I think I will take tomorrow and Friday off. Wanna join me?" I told him that I would do that too. I texted my boss and told her I would be taking Thursday and Friday off too and she texted me right back and told me that was fine. He texted someone. I am assuming it was his boss and then he looked at me and said, "I'm good, how bout you?". I told him I was good too. He spent the night with me and he held me all night. I felt him kissing my back and my shoulders and the back of my neck all night.

We both took Grams out for lunch on Thursday afternoon and we told her that were going away to Nantucket in another week, but we would take her out before we left. Of course, she said we didn't have to, but I insisted and so did Charlie. He told her were leaving next Saturday morning, so we would take her out for dinner next Friday night. She smiled at him and touched his arm and thanked him for being so nice to her. He kissed her on the cheek. Charlie asked her if she wanted to come back to the house for a while and she said she was all set and wanted to go home, so he dropped her off and we walked her to her door. I hugged her and kissed her before I left and so did Charlie.

We went back home and Charlie was a little quiet. "What's wrong Charlie?" He said, "Nuthin' but I have been thinking about how this is going to work if we end up together, which I am hoping will happen. You have your house and I have my house, you know, and shit like that". I touched his arm. "Oh we will end up together. I know that for sure. What we will do is, we will both sell our houses, put our shit together and buy a house together. I have it all figured out." He hit the brakes a little and then pulled over to the side of the road. He put the car in park and then grabbed me and hugged me so tight. "You figured it out already? Does that mean what I think it means? I looked at him and said, "Yes, it means what you think it means and I thought about it right away". "I love you Meggie, more than you can ever understand. You do things to me". He kissed me then pulled back out into the road. We went home and he told me he was taking me out to dinner again at the Terrace View Marina and Restaurant in Spring City. I loved that place and I told him I was happy about that. He dropped me off and walked me in and then said he would be back around 4:00. I went out to water my garden and picked some veggies. I just carried them in. I was afraid to go to the garage after the squirrel. Charlie told me not to leave the garage open too long, because animals will go in there. I walked out to get my mail and my neighbor was sitting on her porch, but I noticed she wasn't looking my way. The lady next door on the right was sitting on her porch too and she was looking in the opposite direction. I guess Charlie scared them both. I was laughing to myself as I walked back to my front door. I decided to sit on my steps too and I was still laughing to myself. I opened my mail while sitting there. It was mostly advertisements and only 2 bills. The electric bill and the gas bill. I sat there for a while and the sun was beating down on me. It actually felt good. Was this why they sat on their front porches? I really didn't give a shit why they were both sitting out there and I am glad that Charlie scared them. Little did they know, I would be selling my house soon. It just made sense to live together. He spent most of his time at my house anyway. I would love to live with him. I walked back into my house and locked my front door and I listened to music and danced in my living room. I was so happy. I put some dirty dishes and cups in me dishwasher and a load of clothes in my washer. Before you know it, it was time to get ready to go out.

I got dressed up in my new sexy bra and underwear and my new dark purple dress with all my new jewelry. It looked so good on me. It was a little shorter than my black dress and it showed a little more cleavage. I got my black clutch and heels out. I put my makeup on and put my hair up. I looked in the mirror and said out loud. "Yup, you look fucking good". I went to the kitchen and sipped on my water bottle while I was waiting for Charlie. He was right on time. He came to the door and peeked into the curtain. It was locked, so I had to go let him in. I peeked back at him through the curtain and he laughed. I opened the door and he looked at me and said, "OMG, Holy Shit. I need to take you to this restaurant more often. You look fucking amazing". I blushed. "Thanks Charlie. This is one of my new dresses. I didn't get to show you what I bought." He said, "I like to be surprised. That dress is definitely you and you wear it well. Ya ready?" I thanked him and told him I was more than ready. He escorted me to the car and locked my door and set my alarm. As we were walking to the car, a male neighbor that lived diagonally across from me, whistled at me and was making remarks and yelling. Charlie said, "Just ignore him Megs". I didn't even look his way, I just got into the car and smiled. He took me to 'our' restaurant, where it really all started, with that kiss. He had reservations this time and he gave his name and the waitress said, "Yes, sir, Mr. Hudson. Right this way". She escorted us to a nice table in the corner of the restaurant and handed us menus and took our drink order. Charlie got his beer and I got my margarita. I looked around and said, "I like this corner. It's nice and private over here and romantic". He smiled and said that he requested this table specifically for that reason. They open at 5:00 for dinner on Thursdays and he called early, so he got the table he wanted. We ordered the Terrace Combo for an appetizer and we shared it. It was Fried Shrimp, onion rings and cheese sticks. I ordered the Shrimp Tacos, which was fried shrimp, served with corn and black bean salsa, homemade slaw and a wedge of lime on two flour tortillas. Charlie said that sounded good so we both got the same thing. It was delicious as always. I loved this place. Their Catfish dinner

was to die for. Actually everything was so good, no matter
what you ordered. We both loved this place. He got up to
use the mens room and didn't want to sit there alone, so I
said I was going to the ladies room. He was standing there
when I came out and walked me back to the table. I sat,
but he didn't. He got down on one knee and proposed to
me. "Meggie, I know we just met and I don't have a lot to
offer you except happiness, but I love you with all my heart
and I would love it if you would be my wife, my love and my
friend for the rest of our lives. Will you marry me Meg?" I
looked at him in shock, but I knew my answer would be
yes, whether it was today or one year down the road. I had
tears streaming down my face and I was shaking, but I
managed to say, "Yes, Charlie, I love you". He put the most
beautiful diamond on my finger and he kissed it and then
he kissed me. He handed me a kleenex. He said, "You
won't be sorry Megs, I promise. I will love you forever and
protect you with my life forever and I will never hurt you."
He was the most romantic man I have ever met. I knew he
was the one a long time ago, before I even met him. I just
had to look at him from my backyard.

We talked through dinner and he asked me if I wanted
dessert here or if I wanted to go for ice cream. I said, "Out
for ice cream, of course". He laughed. We left and headed
to a place called Little Maggie's Ice Cream Parlor. We both
got a soft serve Hot Fudge Sundae and even though I was
full from dinner, I had no problem finishing it. It was so
good. I kept looking at my ring. It was so fucking
gorgeous. I asked him, "Charlie, did you just get this ring
today?" He said, "No, I have had this ring since the day

you said you would date me. I already knew that I loved you and I knew you loved me. When you told me today that you had it all figured out that we would both sell our houses and buy one together, I figured I would take the chance and ask you". I reached over and pulled him to me and we hugged each other. We went home to my house and we sat in the living room together and we kissed and hugged and played around. We got up and went up to the bedroom. I got undressed and hung up my dress and got into comfortable clothes. He wanted me to come to his house, so he drove us around the corner.

9

PLANNING

He went upstairs to change his clothes. He put on jeans and a t-shirt and came down. We sat on his couch. He said, "Ok, so, we have to discuss when we want to get married and when we are going to sell our houses. I am not trying to rush things, but we really should talk about it." I told him that one of us could sell our house now and move in with the other one and that way we would only have one house to sell. We can decide what furniture to keep and what to get rid of and we could put the extra furniture in storage until we found a house to buy. As far as getting married, we need to discuss how fast we want to do this. "I know you never had a wedding and my first one was just a Justice of the Peace at the town hall, so I never really had one either. We don't have to have a big fancy wedding, but if you want that, I wouldn't complain". He smiled at me. "I want a nice wedding. It doesn't have to be over the hill expensive, but I would like to get married in a church in front of God and have a small modest reception. What do you think about a 6 month engagement? Is that too soon or would you rather a year?". I looked at him and said, "One year? No, I would rather the 6 month. I don't want to wait that long". He was so happy with that answer. "Ok, well then lets start planning the wedding and looking for a house and I will put my house up for sale first. I will put all my stuff in storage and move in with you, and after we move into our new house, we can get rid of anything we don't need". He had a nervous laugh. He said, "I know, it seems like we are running to the finish line, but I can't wait to start my life with you Meg. I watched you for 8 years and I yearned for you and now I don't want to wait any longer". I hugged him. I said, "Ditto, I feel the same way. We are not getting any younger and I want a family and I want to be young enough to enjoy this". He smiled and said, "I want to be able to take you on a few nice vacations and enjoy each other. I have money, but I am not a millionaire and I want to spend some on vacations before we start our family". I said, "Oh yes, I know. I don't want a family immediately. We need time to enjoy married life before that happens" He said, "Yes, that was what I was trying to say and if you have any questions or concerns, we should bring them up now. Do you have any Meg?" I told him I didn't, but wanted to know if he had any and he said he didn't. He said, "Ok then it's settled. Wanna call Grams now or wait? I have to call my sister. I have been keeping her updated with our relationship so she knew this was coming." I smiled and said, "Let's call Grams. She will be super happy". I let Charlie call her. "Hi Grams, how are you doing?" She said she was fine. "So Meg and I have some news for you and I hope you will be happy". She was silent. He said, "Grams, Meg and I are engaged to be married. I know this is really soon but there is a story behind this". She screamed, "REALLY? YOU ARE, YOU ARE MARRYING MY MEEGS? THIS IS FANTASTIC. I LOVE YOU CHARLIE". He had her on speaker phone. "MEEGS ARE YOU THERE?" I told her I was here and that she was on speaker phone. "YOU ARE GOING TO BE SO HAPPY, I JUST KNOW IT. I WAS WAITING FOR THIS NEWS". I said, "You were Grams? You knew it was going to happen?" She reiterated her statement. "SO WHEN IS THIS HAPPENING HON? I AM READY FOR IT. I AM PAYING FOR YOUR WEDDING AND I HAVE SAVED MY WHOLE LIFE FOR THIS". I said, "No Grams, you keep your money...." She interrupted me. "DON'T TELL ME THAT. I AM SO EXCITED FOR THIS WEDDING AND I AM PAYING FOR IT. I DON'T WANNA HEAR ANOTHER WORD ABOUT THIS. YOU SET IT ALL UP. I CAN'T DO THAT. I WILL PAY FOR EVERYTHING." I started crying. "Grams. I love you so fucking much. Thank you, thank you. We want to do it right and get married in church in front of God and have a small reception". She said, "I was hoping you would say that. Father Wilson will be happy. You guys set the date and I will let him know and do the church part of it". I heard her sniffling. "Grams, are you crying?" She told me they were happy tears. Then I started crying again because I heard her. Charlie had tears in his eyes. We hung up with Grams and Charlie called his sister and put her on speaker phone. She did not have an iPhone so he couldn't FaceTime her. She answered. "Hi Char, what's up?". He said, "I did it Ang, I did it". She said, "WHAT CHAR, WHAT DID YOU DO?" He said, "I asked Meggie to marry me and she said yes". There was silence for a few seconds. "My baby brother is getting married? OMG. This is fantastic news Char. I am so fucking happy for you. When is the date?" We are going to pick it this weekend Ang. In 6 months or so. We are going to get married in a church and have a small reception here. Will you come?". She yelled, "COME? I WILL BE THERE WITH BELLS ON. YOU BET I WILL BE THERE!" He said, "Ok, I will let you know as soon as we pick a date." They talked for a few more minutes and then hung up. He looked at me and said, "Well, everyone is happy about this, including me". I hugged him and said, "I am happy, really happy too".

So we picked a date. It was going to be Christmas Eve, but we decided before the Christmas Holidays would be better for Angela because she had 4 kids and that would disrupt their holiday. So we picked December 5th. Also, because in early December it was usually in the low 60's and at the end of December it was in the low 50's and got into the 30's at night. Charlie texted Angela and I called Grams to let them know. We got Save the Date cards and he made his list and I made mine. I just had Grams and a few friends. I had no aunts, uncles or cousins. He had his sister, her husband, their 4 kids. His mom and dad had passed and he had an uncle and aunt on his Dad's side with 2 cousins and some friends. So it was a very small wedding and that was fine with us. So, it was going to be about 26 people total. I told Grams not to go overboard. There were only going to be 26 people and if she had any friends that she wanted to invite. She said she had 4 friends that she would like to invite, so there would be about 30 people, give or take. She got Father Wilson and reserved the church for the morning of December 5th at 11:00 a.m. She ordered a limo and flowers for the church.

I ordered the rest of the flowers, blue boutineer for Charlie and my rose bouquet, a wrist band for my Grams and one for Angela and 2 for his nieces. Blue Boutineers for his 2 nephews and one for his brother-in-law. We picked a place called the Old Town Inn on East Tennessee Avenue, in Oak Ridge, for the reception. It was an old Inn that was restored and it had a beautiful and unique venue. It had beautiful landscaped gardens with historic charm. It was perfect for our small reception. We picked a buffet style sit down dinner with appetizers and we picked our cake. Everything was included with the price and you won't believe this, but the total was $3,032.00. When Charlie saw that number, I made a believer out of him. I think all that was left was my gown, shoes, veil and Charlie's tuxedo. I asked Stephanie to be a bridesmaid and Angela to be my Matron of Honor. I told Stephanie to bring her boyfriend and he could be a groomsman, along with Angela's husband (Mike). Charlie had a best friend from work that he asked to be his best man (Joe) and his girlfriend (Julie) would be another bridesmaid. So I had a Matron of Honor and 2 Bridesmaids and Charlie had his best man and 2 groomsman.

Charlie and I went to Nantucket and had the best time. We went on a fishing trip to catch tuna. He did the fishing, not me. We ate a lot of seafood. The lobster up there was fantastic. It tasted so different than Tennessee. We ate so many lobster rolls and baked stuff lobsters and clams and shrimp. You name it, we ate it. We went to a Whaling Museum, we saw the Sankaty Head Lighthouse, we went to a brewery called Cisco Brewers, we saw the Brant point lighthouse. We went to Surfside beach and Madaket Beach. We saw the Loines Observatory that was really interesting. It had two state the art telescopes and astronomers to point things out to us. We went on the steamship authority. We saw a lot of stuff and we stayed at the Nantucket Hotel and Resort. We were given comfy robes and slippers. There was a living room and walk in shower and we were on the pool side. It was a great place and we would definitely go back again. 5 stars from us.

The months were flying by. Charlie moved all his stuff to a storage unit and we had the house professionally cleaned before we put it on the market. It took 5 days and it was sold. Charlie asked for $450,000 and got it. He only paid $150,000, 8 years ago and that is what I paid. We were in a well known area and everyone wanted to live here. I hope I do as well as he did, because we were looking at a house in Brentwood that was really expensive. It was a 5 bedroom, 3 bath home with 4,149 sq ft. It had 2 small rooms up in the attic space too. It had a huge wrap around deck and a pool. Plus it had a long private driveway (away from nosey neighbors) Between his house and mine, that would be a nice chunk down on our house. Plus, I wanted to make it even. Meaning, I wanted to put down exactly what he put down. Charlie had moved in with me a few months ago while we were moving stuff out into the storage unit. All his furniture was expensive and he had nice stuff, so we didn't want to get rid of anything before we found our new house.

We both had birthdays in November and we decided to go out for dinner with Grams and celebrate both of us. We were 2 weeks apart. We went to the Gondolier Italian Restaurant. The food was outstanding and we would definitely go back. We got Fried Mushrooms and Mozzarella Sticks for an appetizer. Charlie got Baked Tortellini with Italian Sausage, I got Baked Cannelloni and Grams got the Baked Cannelloni with sausage. We were so stuffed when we left we had to walk around before we got into the car and we didn't even have dessert. When we got back into the car, I gave Charlie a present. We told each other we weren't going to buy presents, but I couldn't help it. I hope he doesn't get mad at me. He looked at me and laughed and then handed me a small box. I got him a gift certificate to Home Depot and he got me a gift certificate to Amazon. He said, "We might need these when we get our new house". I laughed and told him I was thinking the same thing. Grams was laughing in the back seat. "You two were made for each other".

10

ESTATES

Our wedding was coming up fast. I already had my gown and Steph and Julie had theirs. We sent Angela a picture of their gowns and told her to get whatever she wanted in a shade of the same color. Steph and Julie's gowns were a light shade of blue. Everything was all set. Grams paid the Inn in full. $3,032.00 for all the food, cake and flowers for the tables. Grams told me that she and her 4 friends made all the favors for everyone. I was shocked. "Grams, you thought of everything. Thank you so much. I forgot all about that stuff."

Charlie and I worked every day and came home to eat with each other everyday. This was an important part of our life for Charlie, because he ate alone every single day. We loved each other's company. It was starting to get too chilly to eat on the deck at night, so we started eating at the kitchen table. I would light a couple of candles and make it romantic and then we would have coffee and sit and talk after dinner. I loved this part of my day. Well, other than when we went to bed.

Our wedding day was here and I packed an overnight bag and went to Grams house so he wouldn't see me in my gown before the wedding. His sister came with her family and they stayed at our house. I got to meet her before I left.

They wanted to get a hotel and Charlie said it was not happening. Charlie bought 2 air mattresses for the 2nd bedroom and there was a king size bed in my spare room. He had 2 of his nephews sleep with him in our king size bed. His sister slept with her husband in the spare room and the 2 girls slept on the air mattresses. It worked out. I made sure there was plenty of food in the fridge for everyone and lots of snacks for the kids. They were not staying long after the wedding and Charlie and I were going on our honeymoon immediately after the wedding. Grams offered her second bedroom too, in case we needed it. We were going to Las Vegas for our honeymoon for a week. We both took 2 weeks off so we could re-coup after our honeymoon. Charlie asked me where I went on a honeymoon after my first marriage and I told him that never happened. "What a piece of shit". He was so mad. I told him it was in the past and now I had him to show me what it should have been like. He hugged me and said, "I promised you I would make you happy and I will. I will never hurt you".

The wedding was absolutely beautiful. My Grams picked the most beautiful flowers for the church and it was the most perfect wedding. Father Wilson was so happy to see me. I had my Grams walk me down the aisle and everyone was tearing up. She was so pretty in her light blue dress. She lifted my veil and kissed me on both cheeks, I kissed her back and she put my hand in Charlie's. We exchanged our vows. His sister was crying like a baby. "My baby brother is married". She told Charlie that she had something special for him from his Mom and Dad and he was like, "What are you talking about?". She whispered to him. "Wait till we get to the reception and I will give it to you". He was so puzzled and curious. He told me what she said to him. I was now curious too. What could it be? So we had the limo ride to the Inn and we kissed on the way. He hugged me and said that I made his dream come true.

We got to the Inn and it was all decorated in flowers and our guests were arriving. We had 35 people total. It was perfect. We had a photographer and videographer and they were taking pictures of everyone. It took about 1/2 hour for pictures and I told him I wanted pictures of everyone that came. He did a good job. He got pictures of the food and dancing and each couple and pictures of the table with everyone sitting at the tables. The food was delicious. There was baked ziti, Roast Beef, Baked Chicken Breast and also Beer Battered Cod Fish. There was mashed potatoes, green beans, French fries and Mac and Cheese. I threw the bouquet and Stephanie caught it. We cut the cake and we shared a piece and made everyone believe that we weren't gonna smash it, but at the last moment we did. The whole place filled with laughter. Then we had to go clean it up. There was a DJ that was part of the Inn package and he was really good. I told him I liked Bluesy rock and he made sure he played some. Everyone was having a great time and that made me happy. Grams was sitting with her friends. They ate and they danced together. It was so nice to watch them having a good time. Charlie and I went over to them and we kissed them all and thanked them for coming. Charlie asked Grams for a dance and she started crying. He gave her a Kleenex and he danced with her. That made her day. She handed Charlie an envelope and told him it was the remainder of the money she saved for our wedding and she wanted us to have it for our honeymoon.

Angela came to our table with her husband and they pulled up some chairs to talk to us. She handed Charlie an envelope and said, "Char, this is from Mom and Dad. It's your share of their estate and the only way you could get it, was to get married and I was the executrix, so I had to swear not to give it to you until you got married. I have no idea why they wanted it this way, but I followed their instructions. Do not open it now. Wait till you get home and don't lose it. I got mine when I got married, but I was told not to tell you anything about it, so don't be mad at me." Charlie nodded but he was in shock. He kissed his sister and assured her that he was not mad. Then her husband Mike handed us another envelope with their wedding gift in it. Mike said, "Don't lose this one either and Congratulations" and he chuckled.

Before you know it, it was over and we were on our way home. Charlie gave his sister the extra key to the house and she was going to give it to his friend, Joe, who was going to check the house during the week, while we were gone.

Joe gave us a ride to the house so we could get our luggage and Charlie told him that Angela had the house key and she was going to text him when they were getting ready to leave and he would have to come get it. Joe told him to relax and that everything would be taken care of. We gave Joe the alarm code and we told Angela earlier.

We went upstairs to open the envelope that Angela gave him and also the one that Mike gave us. Charlie opened the estate envelope and I thought he was gonna pass out. He dropped it and started crying. "Megs, we are rich, Megs, OMG. We are rich". I asked him if I could look, because I didn't want to overstep. He handed it to me. "Holy Fucking Shit Charlie. OMG." The Cashier's check was in the amount of $1,350,000.00. We both just sat there on the bed and stared at each other. He said, "Do you have a safe? I can't leave this here without a safe." I told him I had one at my Grams house, but not here. Open the one from Mike. As you recall, Angela told Charlie that Mike was rich and she didn't have to work. He told me to open it. "OMG Charlie, This is fucking unreal." He said, "Tell me". I said, "They gave us $500,000 for a wedding gift. Who does that Charlie?" He said, "My sister and her husband do. I owe her my life". He took the check. It was a cashier's check too. I called my Grams. "Grams, this is important. Really important. She said, "I know, but I wanted you to have it". I said, "No, Grams, listen, we need to come and put something important in my safe". She said, "No I took it out of a trust and I want you to have it". I said, "Grams what are you talking about?" She said, "Did you open my envelope?" She was on speaker and Charlie had her envelope in his pocket. I told him to open it. It was the rest of my mom and dad's estate, $350,000 (my balance) and an additional $350,000. "Grams, What the hell? Where did you get this from?" She told me it was her portion of my mom and dad's estate. I got $500,000 (I used some to buy my house) and she got $500,000. She said, "I paid off my car and house and I paid for your nursing school and that is what is left out of my share. I am well off sweetheart, so I want you and Charlie to have it". I told her what happened with Charlie and his sister and his mom and dad's estate and how he had to get married to get it, and how much they gave us for a wedding gift. "Grams, I need to come and put this money in my safe. When we get back, we will take care of it ok?" She laughed and said, "Honey, you guys are millionaires and yes that will be fine". We just sat on the bed and stared at each other in total shock. I was still in my wedding gown and he was in his tux. Joe yelled up to us and asked if everything was ok. Charlie yelled for him to come upstairs. He was going to tell his best friend. Joe came up and saw our expressions. "What the fuck just happened? Are you guys ok?" Charlie started explaining first about his mom and dad's estate and then showed him the check. Then he showed him the gift from his sister. Then he explained my story about my mom and dad's estate and my grams gift. Joe was stunned. He sat down on the bed next to Charlie and put his arm around him. He was such a joker, but I didn't know him well enough to know this until tonight. He said, "You guys are my bestest friends in the whole fucking world". Charlie started laughing and I busted out into laughter. He said, "You both look like you saw a ghost. Fuck man, you guys are millionaires. You should be screaming at the top of your lungs and be fucking happy about this. You have 2 1/2 million dollars between the both of you. CELEBRATE THE FUCK OUT OF THIS!!! CHRIST, YOU ARE GOING TO LAS VEGAS, GO HAVE A GREAT FUCKING TIME". Joe went downstairs and we changed out of our clothes. I hung my wedding dress in the closet and he hung his tux on the door, so Joe could take it back for him. We didn't say a word to each other. We both got dressed for traveling and we looked up at each other and then I started dancing around the room and I grabbed him to dance with me. "Charlie, we are rich, Charlie we are fucking rich. I want that house we saw. We can pay for it in cash if we want. Plus when we sell this house, we will have almost another million". He looked at me and said, "Well, now I can say, I have money and I will make you happy". I told him, "Charlie Hudson, you make me happy, just being near you. I don't need money to be happy. I only want YOU". He picked me up and twirled me around and said, "Mrs. Hudson, we are fucking rich. You can have anything your heart desires". I told him, "I already have what I want and he is holding me". We took all our wedding gifts and the cashier's checks to my Grams house and put them in my safe. I made sure I gave her extra hugs and kisses. She wished us a good time on our honeymoon and we left.

Charlie and I took off 2 hours later on a plane to Las Vegas. We stayed at a beautiful hotel and we stuck to our budget and did not gamble more than we said we would. I told him that I did not want to change anything in our lives, just because we came into money. Yes, we would have a nice big house and we could afford anything we wanted, but I didn't want our attitudes to change and I wanted everything else the same. He agreed with me. Before he boarded the plane, he called his sister. He thanked them for their extraordinary wedding gift and for the estate money and told them what happened with my parents estate and my grams estate money. His sister was happy for both of us. He told her we had found a house but at the time, we weren't sure we could afford it, but now we could. "You can come and visit and we will have plenty of room".

Our honeymoon was awesome. We did a lot of site seeing and walked the streets and became mesmerized by all the lights on the buildings and blinking signs. It was absolutely beautiful. We went to the casino's, we went to every restaurant and we drank every drink. We did everything there was to do. We took a lot of pictures and sent them to Grams and to his sister and to his friend Joe. There was also a lot of sex. We christened every room in the suite. We ordered in food from room service and breakfasts and drinks. We sat in the whirlpool tub and in the hot tub and we went swimming in the pool and we had a fire pit out back and we napped in a hammock hanging outside our door on the deck. We had a great time together. And then it was over and we were headed back to Tennessee. We kissed all the way back on the plane. Charlie texted Joe when we landed and Joe picked us up from the airport and drove us home and handed us the house key. Charlie thanked him.

11

THE MOVES

Both of our cars were in the garage now because Charlie cleaned my garage out and hung up all the tools so nothing was on the floor except the lawnmower in the corner. He put shelves up out there and had some of his things on them. He checked out the house, the garage and made sure everything was safe. He brought our luggage upstairs and put them in the corner. "We can do this tomorrow right?" I nodded my head yes. He made a call and put it on speaker phone. "Hello?" He said, "Hi Grams, we are home. Just wanted to let you know that we are home and safe". She sighed. "Oh Thank God, Did you guys have a good time." I told her it was really nice. "We did everything." She thanked us for the pictures. We talked a bit and we told her we would come and get her tomorrow and go out to dinner. She was so happy. "Ok, I will be waiting hon".

Charlie and I had a lot to think about. Where were we going to put this money? Should we invest or bury it in the safe. Cash it and take it or invest it, save it? We knew we wanted that house and Charlie called and we put in an offer before it got sold. We still hadn't opened all the envelopes from our wedding either, so there was more. I told Charlie that when we moved into our new house, we needed a big safe that was lagged to the floor, no matter what our decision was for the money. We decided to stash most of it in the safe and invest some in CD's that were giving more than 5% interest in 8 months. We would wait for them to have these specials and then we would open them. He agreed about the safe and it was his idea for the CD's.

We spent the rest of the day, talking about our new life together and our surprise wedding gifts from his parents and from mine. We talked about the house that we put an offer on and how much we would put down on it. We decided not to pay for the whole thing in cash but to have a mortgage we could handle, so we would still have a good credit standing. We ordered some Chinese food and had it delivered and we continued to discuss everything. We also discussed Grams.

We went to Grams earlier in the day so we could finish opening envelopes and see what our total was. And of course, we visited with my Grams. Charlie sat on the couch next to her and put his arm around her and said, "How is my favorite girl?" She put her head on his shoulder and she was in heaven. "I am fine. How is my favorite grandson?" He hugged her. We had discussed yesterday to have Grams come and live with us and Charlie agreed that she should not be alone at her age and that he would love if she did. Charlie looked at her and said, "I have a proposal for you. Think about it before you make any rash decisions. Ok?" She looked at him puzzled. "Meg and I would love if you came to live with us in our new home in Brentwood. At least, we put an offer in on one there and we are praying that we get it. What do you say about that?" Grams looked at me and I shook my head yes. "What do you say Grams. Will you think about it?" She said she would think about it. Charlie said, "Ok good. You think on it, but we would be so happy if you did. When we find out if we got the house, we will take you for a ride there and you can see it before you make your decision. Is that fair?". She hugged him. "Ok young man. That is fair". I think she is going to come with us. The only thing that would keep her from doing it, is her friends, but we can arrange for them to visit and Charlie said he would take her to see them. You know what's really nice about this whole thing? It was all Charlie's idea. He knows how much I love my Grams and that we would be moving a little farther away from her. Charlie told her that he would take her to visit her friends or I would and that they could come visit her. Her face lit up and now she was really thinking. We opened all our wedding envelopes and there was $10,000 more in money. That was a lot of money for only 35 people. Stephanie gave us $500.00 and my boss gave us $1,000.00. Those are big wedding gifts. Charlie's friend Joe gave him $750.00. I don't ever remember people saying they got this much for a wedding gift. When I went to a wedding, I usually gave $200-$250. Charlie's friends gave us most of the money. They were very generous guys. Grams got up to go get ready for dinner. She turned around and said to Charlie, "I really liked that BBQ food you bought from last time. Is that where we are going tonight or do you have another place in mind?" She was so funny. Charlie said, "I know you like that food, and that is why we are going there tonight". She giggled like a school girl and continued to go get ready. Charlie patted the couch next to him and I went over to sit next to him. He whispered to me. "She is a pip". I kissed him and said, "Yup, she is and that is why I love her".

It was about 4:00 p.m. Grams came out. She had combed her hair back and put it in a bun and she had a little makeup on and a clean dress. "I'm ready". Charlie and I got up and he locked up and we took Grams out for dinner. We all got our usuals and they were all delicious. She was smiling from ear to ear. "How is married life you two?" I smiled at her. "I am loving it Grams. Charlie is the best. I love him so much". She looked at Charlie. Charlie said, "I couldn't have made a better choice than Meg. I love her with all my heart and soul and I will take care of her and love her forever." My Grams got tears in her eyes. She said, "I knew you were going to be her husband when I met you, because I loved you too". We had a nice dinner and then we took Grams out for ice cream. She was having so much fun. She thanked us when we dropped her off and Charlie walked her in the house and made sure her door was locked. "Good Night Grams. We love you".

A couple of days went by and we heard from the Real Estate Agent that our offer was accepted. The name of our street was Deepwood Trail. I texted my Grams and told her that our offer was accepted and we were going to make an appointment to go see the house again and we would let her know and she could come with us. Charlie spoke with the realtor and he said we could go see it tomorrow afternoon at 1:00 p.m. I texted Grams and she said she would be ready. Charlie took the cashier's checks to his bank and cashed them. He asked about any CD deals and they didn't have any. They were trying to get him to invest in the stock market and he flat out told them no. "Are you going to leave any here in the bank?" He said, "No I am not". Here is my email. When you have a special going on that pays 5% or more on a CD, let me know. And he walked out. He had his gun on him and had a locked satchel with the money in it. He brought it straight to Grams house and put it in my safe.

That afternoon, we shopped for a safe for the new house. We bought it and told them we had to close on the house before they delivered it. It weighed over 800 pounds. So once it was delivered, it was in its place.

The next day, we picked up Grams and headed to meet the realtor at our new house. Grams walked around and was very impressed. She kept saying "Wow, look at this. Wow look at this". She loved the house and so did we. Grams said, "How come so many bedrooms Meeg?" I said, "Well, Grams, one will be for you, if you want to come and live with us and the other ones will be for our kids and we will need a spare room for when your friends come and visit you". She said, "KIDS, YEAH, Charlie you want kids?". He smiled at her. "Of course I want kids. But not right away. A little ways down the road, but not too far down". He started laughing. She said, "Charlie, you are a good man and you will make an excellent Daddy. I hope I am here to see this". I looked at her and said, "Grams stop talking like that. You are still young and you WILL see your great grandchildren. I have no doubt about that."   Charlie showed her the bedroom that we picked. It had a full bath in it. "This will be our room. You wanna pick yours?" She walked to the end of the hall. Last bedroom on the right and said, "This one. I want this one". He looked at her and said, "So you decided? You want to stay with us?" She said, "I would be a fool to say no. Can you help me sell my house and pack up all the stuff and help me get rid of everything I don't want?" Charlie took her by the hand and said, "You don't have to lift a finger. How's that? Me and Meg will help you and I have a few friends that will help too. We will get you all settled here first and then we will worry about your house ok?" She agreed and then she kissed him. "I love you guys so much".

A week later, we closed on our new house. Once we packed up this one, and had it professionally cleaned, we would put it on the market. Charlie said, "Put it up for $450,00 and we ended up getting that. We started packing. The bedrooms and the bathrooms and the living room and our kitchen stuff. Charlie said, "Just pack it up and I will stack it and we will get movers to bring it over." That was music to my ears. Stephanie offered to come and help and so did Joe and Julie. They stopped at Home Depot for Charlie and picked up boxes and tape and bubble wrap. Charlie had some flattened boxes from his move to my house out in the garage, so he taped those back together and we started using those. The kitchen was the worst with all the glass stuff and pans and dishes and silverware. The bedrooms were easy. I didn't have a lot of junk. I had my dressers, bed, night tables, lamps, clothes.

Ok, it was just as bad. I did have a lot of clothes. We ended up packing for 2 whole days. Everyone was there helping. We had 5 people packing. Steph and Julie did my kitchen and Charlie and I did our bedroom and Joe was in the living room packing all the CD's and stereo equipment and game stuff that Charlie brought. Once he emptied the entertainment center, that was pretty much it. The movers would take the couch, loveseat, tables and lamps. The dining room set was movers and I had a wine rack, and a booze cabinet, that had to be emptied. My outdoor furniture and BBQ was movers, but we had to take the propane tank off. The movers were going to go to the storage unit and empty that out too. Charlie had everything under control. Once the packing was done, the movers would come and then move everything into the new house and figuring out where it would go, would be a pain in the ass. Charlie got a call from the movers. They needed our address and the address where it was going. He gave them my address and then he looked at me and said, "Babe can you look at that closing paperwork on the dining room table and get the exact address of our new house?" I ran over and got the paperwork. I must have looked like a saw a ghost when I looked at it. OMG. "Charlie? It is 3032 Deepwood Trail, Brentwood." He looked at me and said, "Are you fucking kidding me?" I sat in the dining room chair. He gave the address to the mover and then hung up and came over to me and looked at the paper. "Holy Shit Meg. Ok, I believe you now, I do". The movers came and packed up our house and then went to our new house, dropped everything off and went back to the storage unit to

load up Charlie's stuff. They came back to our new house
and Charlie was telling them where to put stuff. He put
post it notes on the bedroom doors. #1, #2, #3, #4 and #5.
Each box had a corresponding number on it. Bathrooms
were numbered too. He was so smart. Kitchen #7. It really
was awesome how he did it. Bedroom #5 was Grams
room and Charlie packed up her clothes and some things
and brought them to our house so the movers could bring
them over. Every door and room had a number on it. Even
the garages had numbers. We had 2 oversized double
garages. Enough for 4 cars. We decided to use one side
for our cars and the other side would be for Grams car,
lawn stuff and his fishing stuff and all the other stuff from
his garage before he moved to my house. The deck was
#12 and the movers were so awesome. They put
everything where we wanted it. Stephanie, Joe and Julie
came to the new house and they helped me and Charlie
unpack. They worked in the dining room and living room
and we now had a sitting room and a game room and a
laundry room. The washer and dryer came with the house,
along with the fridge, stove, dishwasher and a deep freezer
in the garage. We had a walk way that went from the
kitchen door through to the garage and it was all glass. It
was so pretty. I told Charlie I wanted to put some hanging
plants in there to decorate it. The next few days were
hectic. But everyone showed up for 3 days in a row until
we had every last box unpacked. We fed everyone for 3
days. Charlie picked up Grams so she could be with us
and she got to see her room all set up. Her clothes were in
her walk-in closet. She didn't need a dresser anymore, but

we let her keep it, because she wanted it. It was pretty anyway and she found stuff to put in it and she decorated the top of it with a face pot. It is a planting pot of a woman's face and she put fake flowers in it to make it look like hair. It was really cute. I wanted one too. She had her music box for her jewelry. It was really old. I think it was her mother's. And she had a glass snow globe. Whatever she wanted to keep, we let her. Her room was tastefully decorated and looked very pretty when she was done. She was so happy with it. We asked her if she needed anything else and she said, "If I want it, I will buy it. I am sitting pretty too". We bought twin beds for the spare rooms and night tables to match with lamps on each one. We had to figure out where we wanted the safe before the delivery came. At the end of the hall, there was a closet and it had shelves in it. Charlie looked at me, "Do you need this for anything or can we take the shelves out and put the safe in here?" I told him to go for it. He measured and the safe would fit in there perfect. We would be able to open the door without any trouble. He said later on he would put a fake wall behind the door. We got the delivery and Charlie had taken the shelves out of the closet and showed them where to install it. It was a perfect fit. They opened and closed it to make sure. It was really made for it. The delivery men got a nice tip and they left Charlie the paperwork with the combination to the safe. He put the paperwork on top of the safe. They left the door open for him. It comes with a combination, but you can change it if you want. So that was all done. All our boxes were unpacked. We still had some stuff that we didn't know where to put it, but we would figure it out.

All our help left and Charlie gave them each $500.00 for their help. They fought him, but he insisted because they spent 3 days helping us and Steph actually took one day off from work to help.

Grams didn't want to go back to her house until we went to pick and choose what else she wanted to take. Charlie wanted to make her, her own little sitting room where she could have a couch, a TV and a place she could play her music. He got a contractor to take down a wall in one of the oversized bedrooms and we made the bedroom smaller for a guest. She wanted her couch, loveseat, her side table, a lamp. It was a mini living room, so she would have her own space, if she wanted. She was more than welcome to join us in our living room and we made sure we told her that. She had no complaints at all. She asked if she could use the kitchen and cook and we told her to do whatever she wanted to do and she had full access to the kitchen. She had a full bathroom across the hall from her bedroom that we assigned to her. We waited to go to her house until we were fully settled in our new house. We decorated the whole house. We bought new stuff for the extra bedrooms and towels, washcloths, rugs, shower curtains and stuff for all the bathrooms. We bought some beautiful drapes for the whole wall window in the living room. We bought extra outdoor furniture for the deck. It wrapped around the house. Charlie had furniture from his deck and I had some, but it wasn't enough. We bought some pool things. A couple of lounger chairs, pool noodles, some water masks a floating drink holder, a basketball game and some diving rings. We had to hire a pool guy to vacuum and put chemicals. I told Charlie to hire someone to take care of the yard and he agreed that it was too large to take care of by himself. Charlie wanted to hire a housekeeper. He didn't want me cleaning this whole house. It was different with the houses we had, but this place was huge, so I agreed. He did the interviewing and picked a really nice woman. Her name was Lynne and she was about 35 years old. He told her what she would be responsible for and they agreed on a price. Charlie told her that if there was something else he wanted her to do, he would pay her extra and she agreed. So now we had a housekeeper. He asked me if I wanted a maid. "We can afford it Meggie". I said, "No, I want to be normal. I can make beds and clean up after ourselves. Like we have always done. The housekeeper will vacuum and dust and clean the bathrooms and the deck and stuff, but I will do the rest". He smiled at me and said, "Ok, but if you change your mind, let me know". Charlie looked at me and said, "Meggie?" I looked back and said, "What babe?" I was thinking, and I am not telling you what to do, but it's just something to think about. Do you want to stay home and not work? I would love if you didn't have to work. It's something I can give you and it would make me fucking happy". I looked at him and said, "Really? You don't want me to work?" He said, "I am not telling you what to do. If you want to continue to work, that is your decision, but I would love it if you quit and you could stay home. You could get your nails done and go shopping and go out to lunch or just stay home and write or float in the pool. You could do whatever you wanted" I must have looked happy and nothing would make me more happy than to stay home and not clean fucking bed pans and deal with nasty patients. "I wanna quit. Nothing would make me happier than not cleaning nasty fucking bed pans". He came to me, picked me up and hugged and kissed me. "Give your notice. This makes me so fucking happy". I knew it did. He told me many times before we got married that he had nothing to offer me other than happiness and love and now he had this to offer me and I was gonna take it to make HIM happy.

We finished decorating our new house and we bought a lot of new stuff. We had a decorator come in to help us and she did an awesome job. Our new house was gorgeous. I was so happy with it. I saw Charlie standing back and admiring everything too. He was happy too. OOH, that mustache. He turned me on, just looking at him. He told me that he put shelves up in the garage and wanted me to come see. He did a really good job and almost everything was off the floor and he had a couple boxes up high on a shelf. We had a lot of room in the other garage. He said he made room in case Grams wanted to keep some extra stuff. I hugged him.

Charlie hired someone to do the construction for Grams living room and we moved her to another bedroom during the construction. We took her to her house with boxes and she went through the whole house with us and put some things in the boxes. She wasn't keeping too much. She didn't want any of her dishes, but kept a couple of platters that were her moms and she wanted me to have them. She had her recipe book and some food in her freezer, but we threw away everything in her fridge. She had some pots and pans that she wanted me to go through to see if I wanted any and she told me where they came from. She had a little sewing machine and a table that she wanted and that would fit in her sitting room. She had a flat screen TV that Charlie said he would put up for her. She went through everything and told Charlie to get rid of everything else, so Charlie got a junk company and they came and got rid of everything. We had a professional cleaner come in and they cleaned the whole house inside, including all the appliances. It was immaculate. We put it on the market and Grams signed with the realtor. She put it on the market for $250,000. It took 3 weeks and it was sold. She got $228,000 and she was super happy. She put it in our safe and she also put something else in there, but I didn't ask what it was and she had a lawyer come and draw up an updated Will, so that I would get everything when she passed away. She had her own little space in our safe. Oh, so about the safe? The number combination that came with the safe? You guessed it. It was 3-0-3-2 and Charlie couldn't believe it. He said, "You are my soulmate babe. We were meant to be." But he changed the combination, because he said it would be too easy to figure out.

12

BIG SCARE

I put in for my retirement at the medical center. I had a 401K and a pension, so I added that to the safe. My boss said she was waiting for me to do this. "I would do it if I was in your position, but we will miss you terribly".

Now, what was I going to do with myself. First thing to do… I was gonna take Grams out for lunch because I missed a week while moving. I apologized to her and she said, "Are you kidding me right now Meegs? You have done so much for me and we eat together every day. You don't need to take me out anymore. We are always together". I told her, "I want to take you out Grams. Go get ready. We are going". She smiled at me and said, "Ok, you got it". I took her to Buddy's BBQ and we had a great time. Before we left, we ordered some food for Charlie and brought it home with us. He could have it for dinner and me and Grams would have leftover stuffed peppers or salad or a sandwich.

The construction for Grams was done and me and Charlie moved her back into her bedroom and we arranged her sitting room with her couch, loveseat, her table and lamp, her sewing machine. Charlie asked her where she wanted stuff and he moved things around for her till she was happy. She gave him a kiss and thanked him for everything. I changed the sheets in the spare room and got it ready for a guest. Grams said she would wait to have a friend over. She said, "I want to get acclimated here before having someone over". I told her to do whatever she wanted.

My second day off, I made myself a cup of coffee and went out on my deck for the first time. I sat there and enjoyed my coffee. It was a little earlier than I usually get up but I wanted to enjoy the birds and see what it was like out here at this time. I walked around the deck and I was startled by a deer, just grazing on the tree next to our house. Then I saw babies. I took pictures of them on my phone and sent them to Charlie. He must have been busy because he didn't answer. Grams came out to the deck with her cup of coffee and I shushed her and pointed to the deer. She was so excited to see it. We just stood there watching her and her babies for about 10 minutes. Charlie texted me back and asked where that was, so I sent a couple more pictures and told him it was the left side of the house as you drive up to the house. Charlie texted me back and said, "I am on a case right now babe. Talk to you later." I told him to please be careful. So for the rest of the day, all I did was worry about him and Grams knew it. She tried to distract me, but I wasn't having it. I was worried sick about him and I kept tearing up and if anything ever happened to him, I would die without him. Finally, he texted me and said, "I am ok. All done with the case. I know you are worrying about me". I texted back immediately, "Oh Thank GOD, I was worried all afternoon. If anything ever happens to you, I will die without you. Charlie, do you need to work?" He texted back and said, "I don't need to and I was thinking about quitting this job and maybe getting something else, but I am thinking about it". I was relieved that he was ok and I was trying to calm down. I was glad he was thinking about it. Grams asked if I heard from him and I told her he was ok. She seemed to sigh and she was relieved too.

Grams asked me if she could cook dinner tonight. I looked at her and laughed. "More power to you. I would love that". She laughed and said, "Good, because I already started it this morning, while you were out here worrying. I put some baby backs in the crockpot with bbq sauce. I made some Cole slaw and I will make the broccoli that's in the fridge, ok?" I hugged her. "You are the best Gramma a girl could ask for". She hugged me back and said, "He should quit. He doesn't need to do that job". I told her I discussed that with him and he was thinking about it. Charlie came home early and I was waiting for him to come through the door. I grabbed him and hugged him and kissed him and he picked me up. "I am sorry I scared you. I think I am gonna take my retirement. There is no sense in being in danger, when I don't need to work". I was so fucking happy and I started crying. I was holding it in all day and I teared up all day and then wiped my eyes. Now I could let it out. Grams knew I was upset and she checked on me all day. I stayed outside on the deck all day and I didn't eat. He held me and calmed me down. "Come on, let's use our pool. We haven't done that yet". I agreed and we went to get our suits on and got a couple towels out of the linen closet. "Look we have toys to play with babe". And he laughed. I jumped in and it was nice and warm. He did a cannon ball after me and made a big splash and waves. He was a character. I was seeing a lot of him that I never saw before and I loved all of it. We did some swimming and basketball and then we got on the floating chairs. Grams came out with a beer and a margarita and she asked Charlie to give her the drink float. "Wow Grams, you are one heck of a bartender. You are hired. Thank you". I told Charlie she checked on me all day because I was worried and tearing up. "She even cooked dinner Charlie". He said, "I am glad she decided to come live with us. She won't be alone and she will have a purpose in life". He told me that when older people feel like they are needed and wanted, they have a purpose and they live longer. "I will make sure I tell her all the time, how much we need her and that we are so glad she came to stay with us". I took his hand from the floating chair and pulled him so his float was close to mine and we floated side by side together. He drank his beer and I sipped on my margarita. This was a heavenly moment and I won't forget it.

While we were eating dinner, I told Charlie that I thought we needed a garden, but didn't know where we should put it because now we had deer here. He suggested a pot garden on the deck. "A what? What is a pot garden?" He explained that we get big planting pots and fill them with potting soil and we plant in them and leave them on the deck and we can water them right from the deck and the animals can't get to them. We might have to put some wire on the outside of the deck so they can't chew through the slats. "Lets do that. We can go to home depot and get some huge pots and potting soil and some plants and we will make our garden. It's still a little cool at night, so we can cover them with a plastic painters tarp at night". I was excited. "Oh I can't wait. I love to garden and I miss our fresh veggies". Grams spoke up and said, "You guys go ahead. I will clean up the kitchen. It's not much to do." I said, "Grams, we can help and then we will all go, if you want". She smiled at me. "No, you go. I want to learn where everything goes and I can't do that, unless I do it". We agreed with her and asked her again before we left but she said she was fine.

We took Charlie's car because he had a big back seat and a huge trunk. We got there and they had a huge selection of plastic pots, plants and tons of potting soil. We had to get a flat bed carriage because of the soil. We needed a ton of it. Charlie got 10 bags. He said if we didn't need it all, that we could use it next year, but he thought we needed all of this. We got a lot of pots and then we went to the plant section. We got cherry tomatoes, Campari tomatoes, some heirloom tomatoes, cucumber, Red pepper, purple pepper, yellow pepper, cubanelle peppers, zucchini, spaghetti squash, a watermelon and few other things. Charlie said he wanted to try and build a garden in the yard. He said it would look like a cage and be all wired and have a gate. "We can put the larger plants down there. Like the zucchini, spaghetti squash and the watermelon. It doesn't have to be huge, but big enough for these plants." He got some wood, nails, wire and a latch for the door. I laughed. "I hope we can fit all this in the car". He laughed and said, "I hope so. I wasn't thinking about that. If it doesn't fit, we can rent a truck to get it home and then come back for the car. As a matter of fact, that is what we are gonna do. Why worry about it?". So he picked up some extra wood and wire and then we walked around the store to see if there was anything else we needed. He got some white paint and a few other things. We told the cashier that we wanted to rent a pick up truck to get it home and she arranged for that. We packed up the truck and drove all the stuff home. We unloaded it into the garage and then we drove back to Home Depot to get his car.

We got home and saw the front door open. Charlie got out of the car and said, "STAY HERE". He ran up to the door and pulled his gun out and yelled for Grams. "WHERE ARE YOU GRAMS?" There was no answer. I sat in that car and started bawling my eyes out. "Grams, grams". Charlie went into the house with his gun drawn and kept yelling for her. "GRAMS, GRAMS?" He walked out back and she wasn't on the deck. The kitchen was still a mess, like she was interrupted. He walked through every room and then he got to her room. She was in her chair and panting. She was out of breath. He knelt down next to her and said, "Tell me what's going on. Are you feeling ok?" She said she couldn't breath and she had a pain in her chest. He ran out to me and said, "Call 9-1-1. I think Grams is having a heart attack. DON'T FREEZE MEGS, JUST DO IT." I didn't freeze I called them right away and gave them the address. They were on there way. I ran into the house while I was on the phone. I ran for the medicine cabinet and got the baby aspirin. I gave her 4 of them and told her to chew them. Charlie picked her up and laid her down on the bed and put a pillow under head. I heard the ambulance and went out to meet them. They came in and followed me to her room. I told them that I gave her 4 baby aspirin to chew and that I was a nurse. The EMT shook his head at me and said, "You probably just saved her life." We gave them all her information. Charlie wanted to go in the ambulance with her and told me I would be better off driving my car to the hospital and I would be less hysterical. "If you can't drive, then come with me". I told him I could drive. He held her hand the whole way to the hospital. They had her on oxygen and they were monitoring her oxygen intake and taking her blood pressure I met them there. I was right behind the ambulance with my blinkers on and I kept up with the ambulance and I didn't give a shit if I got a ticket for speeding. They rolled her out of the ambulance and Charlie was right there, running with the EMT's and holding her hand. She was admitted as soon as she got there. I sat at the desk and gave them the information that they needed and went to see her. Charlie was still holding her hand. I was holding her other hand. She was awake and said, "I am not going anywhere yet. Stop your shit". She was a feisty old lady. She didn't want anyone to fuss over her, but I didn't care. I was still gonna hold her hand. I kissed her on her cheek and said, "Bet your ass, don't you even think about going anywhere". I was tearing up so I turned my head away from her. She looked at Charlie and said, "Quit your job hon, we don't need to worry about you". That is all Charlie had to hear. He thought that he caused her heart attack. I knew that's what he was thinking and right away I said, "This is not your fault, don't you even think that". He looked at Grams and said, "I am retiring from that job as of this moment". She smiled at him. She was all hooked with monitors and there was beeping and swooshing. I knew what they were and what they were doing, but Charlie didn't and he was asking me what each one does and I explained all of it. They came to take her for a test and then brought her back. About an hour later, they asked to talk to us outside of the room. Grams had a blockage in her right coronary artery and they were going to install stents to open her artery up. They said she would be fine. They took her to surgery and she came back 3 hours later and she was fine. We had to wait till she woke up from the anesthesia. She was talking and was in good spirits. She said, "I told you I am not going anywhere". Charlie kissed her cheek and said, "You better not, we need you. The fucking kitchen is still dirty" And he laughed. She smiled at him. She told him she opened the front door so we would know something was wrong and that she couldn't yell to let him know that she heard him. Charlie told her not to worry about anything. "You just get your ass home. We can't live there in that big house without you". She was drifting off to sleep, so we told her we were going home and that we would be back tomorrow.

Charlie and I went home. We locked up and set our house alarm. We both cleaned up the kitchen and then went to take a shower. Our new shower in our bedroom was huge. You can bet that we had some great sex in there. We dried off and got into bed and snuggled down deep into the comforter. We bought cushy comforters with big fluffy pillows and you actually sunk into it and nobody would see you. Well, I am exaggerating slightly, but you get the idea.

We turned on the TV and we were kissing and hugging. Charlie said, "Grams is gonna be ok Meggie. This was an awful scare, but you were quick thinking and I am proud that you didn't freeze".   I told him that, that was my job. "It's what I was taught. You can't freeze or you will lose a patient. My nursing just kicked in. I know she will be fine. She is in good hands. They won't keep her long. Maybe just tomorrow and then they will let her come home". He looked stunned. "Really? She just had a heart attack". I told him that with today's medicine, you are in and out. "She will have to rest at home". He said, "We are getting a 24 hour nurse for her and don't say no, because I am doing it".   I smiled at him. "She is your grams too, so you do whatever you want, but I will be here". He told me he was doing it and I let him. He loved my Grams like I did and I loved him more for that.

Charlie called his boss the next day and told him he was going to take his retirement and told him what happened with my Grams. His boss was upset, but understood and told him that he would get his paperwork ready. Charlie had about 12 weeks vacation, because he kept rolling it over and he asked his boss, if he could take it. His boss said that he would be getting a check for the total amount of those weeks. Charlie was worried that he would lose that time, but his boss assured him that he wasn't losing anything. He told his boss that he wouldn't be in today but would come in tomorrow to fill out the paperwork.

We went to visit Grams and she was doing well. The doctor wanted her to get up and go to the bathroom, so the nurse helped her get there. Charlie was at the nurse's station getting information about a 24 hour nurse. They helped him and said Grams would be coming home tomorrow and the nurse would be available immediately. He told them that we had a room for the nurse. They informed him that it was gonna cost him because a full time nurse was not covered under her insurance. He told them it wasn't a problem.

We stayed for a while and told Grams we would come and get her tomorrow because she was coming home. We kissed her and hugged her. Before we left, I said to Charlie, "I wonder if Stephanie would consider coming to take care of Grams?" He looked at me like a light bulb went off. "Text her now before we leave here". I texted her and told her what happened and she told me she wasn't working at the hospital anymore and that she would love to take the job. Charlie told her she would have to stay overnight and that he would pay her $3,000 to stay for a week. She took the job, so Charlie went to the nurse's station and cancelled the nurse and told them that I had a friend that was a nurse and she was going to do it. So it was all set. I asked Steph why she wasn't working at the hospital and she said, "Things have changed there Meg. Our boss got let go and then I got my walking papers because they said they were downsizing" I was shocked. "OMG. Really Steph? That's horrible". She told me she got a severance package and she left. She told me she broke up with her boyfriend. I said, "You did? Why?" She told me she would tell me another time. I told her I would need her starting tomorrow. She said she would come tonight and get settled in and Charlie said that would be fine. Charlie told her to come for dinner and she agreed. I looked at him and said, "Oh God, I didn't plan anything for dinner". He smiled at me and said, "That's fine. I was gonna order in anyway or we can go out". I told him to order in because I wasn't in the mood to go out. He told me he didn't feel like going out either. He looked at me and said, "Meggie, you don't need to cook every night. There is no need for that. We can order in or go out whenever you want. If you want to do it every night, so be it". I looked at him and said, "I love you Charlie Hudson". He said, "I love you more Meg Hudson".

13

GRAMS IS HOME

So Stephanie showed up with a suitcase and we showed her the room next to Grams. She said she could sleep on her couch to keep an eye on her. Charlie asked if she wanted the twin bed moved in there. She shrugged her shoulders so Charlie moved the twin bed from the next bedroom into Grams room. Steph said that way she would be there if anything happened. Charlie agreed with her. We took a poll on what to eat for dinner and ended up getting a shit load of Chinese Food.   We ate outside on the deck. The weather was perfect for it. I told Steph to bring her bathing suit and she did. We cleaned up dinner and Charlie came out and did a cannonball into the pool and scared the shit out of me. Steph was hysterical. She ran to get her suit on and I did the same. We had so much fun that night. He played basketball and dove for the rings and of course Charlie won. He got the most at one time. We were floating on pool noodles and talking. Charlie got out and made us Margaritas and got himself a beer. "Where is Grams when we need her?" I laughed and told Steph the story. She said, "Aww, Meg, that is so sweet. I love your Gramma". Charlie put the pool lights on and we continued to party until about 10:00. Charlie went in to use the bathroom and on his way out, he saw something in the microwave and opened it up. Grams had made a yellow cake with chocolate frosting. When the hell did she do this? It could have been during the day when I was outside on the deck all day. He cut 3 pieces and made some coffee. He put everything on a tray and brought it out. We got out of the pool and wrapped ourselves with a towel and sat at the round table with the umbrella and had cake and coffee. "Thanks Grams". We all said it. It was so good after being in the pool and drinking. Charlie told us that she had it in the microwave. We brought everything inside, Charlie turned off the pool light and closed up the slider and locked it. Steph said good night and went to Grams room and she said she was gonna watch some TV. Charlie and I sunk into our cushy comforter and pillows and turned on the TV and fell asleep about 2 hours later.

We got a call from the hospital that Grams was going to be released at 1:00 p.m. Charlie got up and made breakfast for everyone. He fried bacon and sausage, made toast and scrambled eggs and coffee. Steph came out of Grams room, rubbing her eyes and said, "OMG, what smells so good?" Charlie said, "Your breakfast". She said, "You sure you only need me for a week?" And she laughed. She set the table for Charlie. I was in getting dressed. I came out and got the napkins, creamer, sugar and spoons out. He put everything on platters and put it on the table and we all helped ourselves. I said, "Thanks Babe. This is really nice and it's delicious. Steph thanked him too. Charlie told Steph that Grams was going to be released at 1:00 and we would be going to get her. She asked if she could come and she would sit in the backseat with her. Charlie told her she could. Steph and I cleaned up the kitchen and Charlie went to the garage. He was always puttering around in there. Actually, I think he was building the box for the garden out back. He said he would need my help bringing it out back. It was just a wood frame and not heavy, just awkward. He was going to anchor it to the ground and put the fencing around it and put the door on it when that was done. He came in the house and we were just wiping down the table and finishing up. "Can I get both of you to help me bring this garden box around to the back?" We went into the garage and we helped him carry it to the back of the yard. He was hammering stakes into the ground. We were both standing there watching. The wire was in a big roll. He had gloves on because it had sharp edges. He threw me a pair of gloves and I put them on. He unrolled some of the wire and asked me to hold it still. He stapled the wire into the wood frame, all the way down and then unrolled more and did the same thing, all the way around. He attached the door with hinges that were already screwed in. He brought the wire, right up to the door and stapled the last of it into the wood. He cut the rest of the wire roll off and stapled the ends in so no one would get hurt. Then he went inside the pen, and he dug out the grass and put it in a barrel and then he turned the soil over. He brought the barrel to the end of the driveway with the rest of the trash and came back with the plants that we bought. The zucchini, the watermelon, the spaghetti squash, the cucumbers and the heirloom tomatoes. He planted them and then brought the hose down there and watered them. I was so proud of him because he finished it and he was so handy. It was 11:45 so he came in to shower and get ready. We left at 12:30 to get Grams. She was up and dressed and the nurse was brushing her hair and put it up in a bun for her. We brought her a pair of shoes because when she left she didn't have any on. She saw Steph and said Hi to her. Charlie told Grams that Steph was going to be her nurse for a week. Surprisingly, she did not argue at all.   She just smiled at Steph and said, "Thank you honey". We signed her out of the hospital and she was thanking all the nurses. They put her in a wheelchair and wheeled her out the front door and then Steph took her by the arm and helped her into the back seat. I thanked the nurse for her help and we left. Grams was very talkative. She and Steph were having an in depth conversation back there. Charlie just looked at me and smiled. "This was a good idea Megs". I shook my head and grabbed his right arm and hugged it. I loved this man with all my heart and he was right in my own backyard the whole time. That mustache. OMG.

We got home and Steph got Grams comfortable in her room. She wanted to sit up for a while. Charlie bought her a recliner and she sat in that to watch TV. Steph gave her a piece of cake and a decaf coffee and set up a tray next to her. Steph took her blood pressure every hour the first day and she was very attentive to the pills she needed to take. I was in an out all day checking on her. Charlie said he was ordering food in so he told me not to worry about dinner. It's a good thing, because cooking dinner was not on my list of things to do lately. I was so preoccupied with Grams, even though I had Steph, I was still worried. I knew her day was coming and no matter what I told myself, I would never be prepared for that day. She was 75. That is still young, I know that, but I still would not be ready when it happened. I think Charlie knew I was thinking bad things. He came up behind me and hugged me. "You ok Meggie? I see steam rising, which means you are thinking". I laughed at him. "Yeah, you are right. I know Grams is gonna be ok, but I will never be ready when she decides to leave". He said, "I knew you were thinking bad things. You have to stop thinking about it, especially since you know you won't be ready. No one is ever ready, so stop thinking about it. You will drive yourself crazy Meggie". I turned around to face him. He tilted his head and bent down to give me a kiss. Oh God, he is so fucking handsome and that fucking piece of beard is driving me nuts. I kissed him long and hard and he knew I was getting hot. He said, "What do you want to eat tonight? Mexican? Italian? BBQ? Sushi?" That was it. I told him I wanted Sushi. "Let me go ask Steph if she likes Sushi". He told me that if she didn't, they had other stuff on the menu that wasn't sushi. I walked into Grams room and Steph was sitting on her couch and Grams was sleeping in her recliner. I took the coffee cup, dish and fork out and asked Steph. She said she loved Sushi. I gave her a thumbs up, so I wouldn't wake up Grams. I told Charlie she liked Sushi, but we needed to get Grams her favorite that wasn't sushi. He shook his head and went out on the deck to peek at the garden and I followed him. "Wanna plant the pots?" I told him that I wanted to get them done. We both went to the garage and we started bringing stuff out to the deck. He said he would carry the potting soil because they were heavy. I told him to use the wheel barrow. "You are brilliant. Why didn't I think of that?" He piled 3 at a time on the wheel barrow and started loading them on the deck. I carried all the rest of the plants out and the big pots and put them on the deck. Charlie slit open a bag and he had a shovel and started filling the pots. As he filled them, I planted the plants and started lining them up on the deck. He finished filling the pots and then he had the wire roll in the wheel barrow and he stapled wire to the side of the deck rails so no chewing would happen from the deer. "I hope this works". I laughed. "It will unless they come up on the deck." He gave me a horrified look. "OMG, you know that could happen. Unless I put a gate at the top of the deck, right there" and he pointed to where he would put it. "I have the wood, but I would have to figure this out." He was shaking his head. "The things we have to do to get some fresh vegetables". He started laughing. "We will figure it out." He got his measuring tape out from the garage and put all the extra soil away and I carried the pots we didn't use back to the garage and got a broom to sweep up the mess we made. Charlie measured for the gate and wrote it down on a piece of paper, while I swept the dirt off the deck and cleaned everything up.

Charlie placed the order for Sushi and we went out on the deck and looked at our work. He watered the plants that I put in the pots. I went to check on Steph and Grams. Grams was awake and she was talking to Steph. "Hi Meegs. I am feeling pretty good. I wanna take a walk". Steph told me that she just walked her around the room and she shouldn't do too much. "Grams, you just went for a walk around the room. You have to take it easy for a little bit ok?" She started to cry. "But I wanna walk out to see Charlie". I said, "Don't cry Grams. I will have Charlie come in here, how's that? You are gonna come out and sit with us at dinner and you will see him there too. Ok?" She said ok. I went to get Charlie. "You are being summoned. Grams was crying because she wanted to take a walk to see you and Steph made her walk in her room." He ran down to her room. "Here I am, did you miss me Grams?" She put her arms out for a hug. She loved my Charlie so much. He went to her and hugged her. "Our dinner is gonna be here soon and you can come and eat with us ok?" She shook her head. He sat on the floor next to her chair and talked to her until the dinner came. I got the order and carried it into the dining room. Charlie got Grams out of the chair and helped her to the dining room chair. Steph followed and she whispered to me. "She loves him". I told her I knew that from day one when she met him. I asked Steph, "How is she? Is she acting ok and is her blood pressure ok and everything". Steph told me that she was a little emotional, but blood pressure was fine and she was being cooperative. I shook my head. "Good, there is nothing worse than an uncooperative patient and she can be a handful to get her way. I know this from experience". She laughed and said she could handle her.

We had a nice dinner and Grams was very sociable and talking with Charlie the whole time. He looked at me a few times and I just smiled at him. I texted him at the dinner table and said, "She fucking loves you so much". He texted me back and said, "I know, I love her too". Steph caught on to what we were doing and she texted Charlie from under the table. "Stop texting about your Grams. LOL". He excused himself and said he had to answer his text from Joe. He went in the bathroom and he was laughing. He came out and he was laughing. "Joe is so fucking funny". I said, "Oh, what did he say?" He gave me a look as if to say he was gonna kick my ass later. Steph was laughing under her breath. Charlie said, "Oh, I will tell you later. It is about my retirement".   He got up and said, "Anyone want a margarita?" I told him coke was fine and Steph said she wanted a coke too. "Grams, what do you want to drink?" She said, "Um, how bout some water?" Charlie got her a bottle of water and opened it for her. She smiled so sweet at him. I felt so bad now that we were texting back and forth. What if she knew and thought we were making fun of her. We weren't, I swear. I would never do that. I loved my Grams too much to do that. We finished up eating and Grams was still talking to Charlie and he told her that we planted the garden on the deck and out back in the yard. "Do you want to see it?" She said she wanted to, so while Steph and I were cleaning up, he took her out on the deck and walked her around to the side of the house and showed her all the plants and then they walked to the other side and pointed out in the yard and showed her the garden box that he built. She was happy and she was holding onto his arm. "You have been working hard around here to make it nice for my Meegs. You are a good man, Charlie". He walked her back into the house and told her that she had her walk and now it was time to settle in bed and to listen to Steph and do whatever she needed to do. She said she would. Steph took her

arm and walked her down the hall to the bathroom and she
gave her medicine and washed her up and got her into her
nightgown and put her in bed. She had the TV on for her
and she had a bottle of water on her nightstand. Steph
stayed in there for the rest of the night and kept an eye on
Grams and when she went to sleep, she turned the TV
down so it wasn't that loud and she had the timer on so it
would go off by itself.

14

REALLY BAD WEATHER AND WATER PROBLEMS

Charlie and I got frisky in the shower, as usual, and then we settled into our cushy bed and watched TV until we fell asleep.All of a sudden, our phones were going off and I heard Steph's phone going off. It was the alarm for a tornado warning. Charlie jumped out of bed and read the announcement. He put the weather channel on to see what was going on. He grabbed me and went down to Grams room. He yelled to Steph. "COMING IN". He grabbed Grams and carried her to the bathroom across the hall. It had no windows. He yelled at Steph. "GET IN THERE WITH HER, NEXT TO THE WALL, MEGS YOU GET IN NEXT TO GRAMS". He ran across the hall and grabbed 2 twin mattresses, one at a time and he handed me and Steph the first one and we put it over all our heads and then he brought the other one and he got in the shower and put it over our bodies and he covered everyone with a mattress. "DON'T FUCKING MOVE. STAY RIGHT HERE NO MATTER WHAT HAPPENS".   Poor Grams had no idea what was going on. She was sitting in the shower stall with Steph next to her, then me and Charlie and we were covered with mattresses. We all had our phones with us and the alarms were going off again to take cover. There was a line of tornadoes heading straight for us. I was trying not to cry, but my tears were leaking out and I grabbed

Charlie and held on tight. He was hold me tight and kissing me. "This is the safest place for us Megs, no windows". He held me tight to comfort me. I was so fucking scared. I don't think I have ever been this scared in my life. Steph was holding onto Grams and we heard things hitting the house and there was a lot of wind and we could hear the rain hitting the roof. We were in the shower for one hour and then it was over. Thank God it didn't hit us. It might have gone around us, but we couldn't see anything because it was 2:00 a.m.. Charlie moved the mattresses out and put them back on the beds. I was trying to get up, but I couldn't move. He gave me his hand and lifted me out. He did the same for Steph and then he reached in and grabbed Grams and carried her back to her bed. He was my protector. He was our protector. He took charge and knew what to do. He took my arm and said, "Let's go back to bed and pray there aren't anymore alerts tonight". I held on to him tight, all night. I didn't let go of him. I was still scared it was going to happen again. I was tearing up and ready to cry and I was still shaky. "You are ok Megs. You are ok". Most tornadoes that hit in Tennessee were during the night. I think because of the humidity or something.

I finally dozed off but it wasn't a sound sleep and Charlie was still holding me. We got up around 7:00 because we wanted to see the damage. We walked downstairs and Charlie stopped before he hit the bottom. "Stay there Megs. We have a problem." The whole downstairs was flooded. There was water everywhere. He didn't know where it was coming from. He stepped into the water and started walking around to see if he could see where it was coming from. I was talking to him. "Be careful Charlie, don't slip on the tile. Please be careful". He said he was ok. A few minutes went by and he said, "I FOUND IT. THE PIPE BURST UNDER THE KITCHEN SINK. I TURNED THE WATER OFF".   He called a plumber and called the insurance company and put in a claim and they sent out someone to clean up the water and dry everything up. He opened the front door and water started spilling out the door. He opened the slider in the back and water was spilling out on the deck. He said, "Oh God, we need all new plants babe. They are all over the deck. From what I can see, though, the plant box protected the big plants. They look fine." I took a few towels out of the linen closet, but Charlie made me put them back.   Charlie got the wet-dry vac from the garage. When he opened the door, the water started pouring into the garage, so he opened the garage door to drain it out of there. I couldn't believe how much water there was. Charlie said the water must have been running for hours. There must have been 3 feet of water. We were going to have to replace floors and our new living room furniture and tables, the dining room table, was ruined. The kitchen table and chairs were all wood and they were ruined. The cabinets in the kitchen had water lines. They were all ruined. Everything we had down there was ruined. The tiles were all lifting and they had to be replaced. We had a big fucking mess. I can't believe that we have only been in our new house for 4 weeks and this happened. Thank God we had insurance. It was going to be a pain in the ass while everything was being repaired. Charlie did his best drying up the water with wet-vac and used some towels. The next day, the insurance adjuster came out and gave us an estimate. All the doors on that floor had to be replace too. Basically the whole bottom floor, including all the furniture had to be replaced. The insurance adjuster hired someone to come and lift all the tiles off the floor in the whole bottom floor in the house and they put fans everywhere to dry everything. The plumber came and fixed the pipe under the sink, so we could use the water. Charlie ordered food for everyone for every meal. He didn't want me in the kitchen cooking. Charlie said the insurance quote was good but they were aware that it may go over. They had to determine whether the sub-flooring was ok to tile over. We picked out all our new furniture, again, but delayed delivery until the tile was installed. We got a new kitchen set, a new living room set, new dining room table and new side tables. We had to get all new kitchen cabinets because the bottom ones were soaked with water and they couldn't match the top ones, so all of them had to be replaced. Our gas stove had to be replaced because the water went too high and ruined the insides. We needed a new refrigerator and a new dishwasher. The insurance company that we had was awesome. They covered everything. We had $1,000 deductible. We had to replace the area rug in the dining room and living room and the little rugs in front of the sink and stove and the entrance to the slider. You can't even imagine what had to be replaced. You don't realize it until everything is under 3 feet of water. But it was quicker than I thought and everyone did their job. We had the plumber look at all the connections in the whole house, so this wouldn't happen again. He changed the connection to one of the toilets upstairs and another one under the sink in the downstairs bathroom. That part wasn't covered, but the guy was really nice and agreed to do it. Charlie paid him for his work. Charlie went to Home Depot and got all new plants for me and came home and planted all of them. I hugged him when he took me out to see what he did. "I love you so much Charlie Hudson". We walked down to the back where we had the garden box and looked at the zucchini and stuff and it was fine. It looked like the wind didn't even touch it. We had little zucchini's growing and flowers on the watermelon plant, the heirloom tomatoes and the spaghetti squash. Charlie said, "I should build another big garden box and put everything else in there instead of the pots on the deck. Maybe next season we will do that". He bought deck boxes and some pretty flowers and he planted them all along the top of the deck. It looked so pretty. The insurance company had to add $20,000 to our claim and they paid for everything. I was very pleased with them. Steph stayed to help with Grams for 3 weeks while we were having the house done. She didn't need it, but I was busy and didn't have the time to give her any attention. Charlie paid her well and Steph was comfortable. Charlie moved the bed from Grams room back into the spare room and Steph slept in her own room. Grams was back to normal and walking around and showering herself and dressing herself. Steph was here for company and someone to talk to. Charlie and I were so busy. We had to pack up the whole kitchen again, so we could have the cabinets taken down and the new ones put up and then we had to unpack the boxes and put everything into the new cabinets. Finally, we were done with everything and we had all the new furniture delivered.

Charlie had the landscapers come and clean the whole yard. There was debris everywhere. We had someone's umbrella in our backyard, but our closet neighbor was blocks away. He put it out by the mailbox and someone came to take it.

We were finally back to normal. I started cooking meals again and I loved having Charlie home. I think Charlie loved being home too. We always had plenty of things to do around the house. He took care of the garden and flowers. He took care of the stuff in the garage. He washed and waxed all the cars, even Grams car. We had to have a conversation with Grams about her car. We took her everywhere and we didn't want her to drive anymore. Charlie said he would have the conversation with her because she would listen to him.

So tonight I made Chicken Parmesan and Spaghetti with salad and garlic bread. Steph was impressed. "Wow Meg, you really know how to cook. This is awesome". Charlie looked at her and said, "Why do you think I married her?" He started laughing. Steph laughed and said, "I knew it". Grams started laughing with us. "I taught her how". I was sitting next to her and patted her on the back. "Yes, you did Grams. You taught me everything. You are the best gramma ever". Charlie was sitting on the other side of her and said, "Grams, I want to talk to you about something."

She looked at him and didn't say anything. "Since you are living here with us and we take you everywhere you want to go, I was thinking that you should sell your car. I just don't think it's safe that you drive anymore. Are you on-board with this?" She looked at me and then looked at Charlie and she said, "That sounds good to me. You guys take good care of me and I don't need to drive. Feel free to sell my car and I want you guys to take the money for it. I don't need anything and whatever I need, you guys give it to me". Charlie gave her a hug and said, "Whatever you need, you just ask. If you want to go somewhere for anything, just ask and we will take you". She said, "Ok, no arguments from me. I'm Good". Charlie told me later that he had a buyer for the car before he even asked her. Her car was only 4 years old and it was like brand new. It only has 6,000 miles on it. The guy that wants it said he would pay $22,000 for it. "We will put that money in an envelope in the safe with her name on it, so if she wants to spend it, she can. I knew she wouldn't give me a hard time". He laughed. "I will wait a couple weeks before I sell it to him. It doesn't even have any dust or dirt in it. It's like brand fucking new." So that was that and now I didn't have to worry about Grams driving anywhere. Steph left after 3 weeks and Charlie paid her very well and she was happy.

15

ITALY HERE WE COME

So now we were really back to normal. It was just the 3 of us. We had a whole new downstairs. Our garden was giving us a bunch of vegetables. We went swimming and we even got Grams in the pool to float around. She enjoyed herself so much. Charlie moved her around the pool and kept a close eye on her. When she was done, he picked her up and carried her out of the pool, wrapped her in a towel and helped her to sit in the chair. He came back in and we were playing basket ball and diving for the rings. We had so much fun that day. We got out and we helped Grams go upstairs. We didn't want her to slip. She went in her room and changed her clothes and came back out and I found her sitting in our living room downstairs. "It's so nice in here". I said, "Enjoy Grams. Do you need something to drink?" She said she wanted a bottle of water and she started to get up. I told her to stay put and she said she didn't want to spill anything in there. "Relax, Grams, it's water." She sat back down. "Do you want a snack before dinner?" She said no.

Grams had a follow-up appointment with her cardiologist today at 2:00 p.m. We took her out for breakfast first and then to the mall and she went into her favorite store and she bought herself a few new dresses, a couple pairs of pants and blouses, a new nightgown, a pair of slippers, a jacket and a bottle of perfume. Charlie carried her bags to the car and we took her to visit one of her friends. We dropped her off for an hour and then went back to pick her up. She was smiling and so happy. We took her out for lunch and then headed to her appointment. They did an EKG and checked her blood pressure and her oxygen intake. The doctor said she was healthy as a horse. He refilled her prescriptions. He looked at her and said, "You have some very special people taking care of you". She put her head on my arm and reached for Charlie. Charlie came to her side and she hugged his arm. "Yes, I do. I really do". The doctor smiled at both of us. "Whose gramma is this. You are both so attentive, it's hard to tell". I raised my hand. "Keep doing what you are doing. She seems very happy and she is very healthy". Grams got a clean bill of health. We made sure she did some walking and had exercise daily and she ate good food. We did take good care of her.

Charlie and I were married 6 months now and he wanted to take me on vacation for 2 weeks, so we asked Steph to come and take care of Grams. She jumped at the chance to do it because she still wasn't working. She wasn't able to get another job yet. She had interviews and stuff, but nothing ever panned out for her. Charlie gave her Joe's number for an emergency contact and he told Joe what we were doing and that he was on-call.

We decided to go to Italy and see Rome, Venice, Naples, Tuscany, Florence, the Leaning Tower of Pisa, do a bike tour, a Gondolas ride down the canals of Venice, a wine tour, the beach and museums. We were gonna do as much as we could in 2 weeks. I was so excited for this trip. We hadn't been away in a while. Steph came and we left for our trip. It was a 12 hour flight to Rome. We had first-class seats and even though it was a long flight, we enjoyed it. We ate and had drinks and we talked and played card games and took a nap. We were on the go, for the whole trip, because we wanted to fit everything in. We ate at all the restaurants and we drank at pubs and we saw the colosseum in Rome and the Gondola ride was so romantic with all the lights and music. We visited the wine countries in Tuscany and did a wine tasting and bought a few bottles. We did a bike tour and cycled through the streets and villages. I will tell you that I haven't ridden a bike for ages and my legs felt like rubber for 2 days after. We went to a few beaches. God they were so friggin beautiful. We saw the leaning Tower of Pisa and we took pictures in front of that. It was absolutely amazing. Charlie and I really enjoyed this vacation. We stayed at Villa Ambra. Its had 59 acres of grounds and it was in the Tuscan countryside. It had an outdoor pool and it produced its own olive oil and wine. Our room was decorated in light colors and the furniture was all light wood. It had a restaurant as well. The two weeks flew by so fast, but we enjoyed every minute of it. Charlie makes everything fun anyway. No matter what we are doing, he makes me laugh.

There were no emergencies at home. Steph and Grams even went out for dinner a couple of times together. Grams insisted she pay for Steph. They went out for ice cream and did some grocery shopping. Grams loved Steph and they both got along so well.

We showed them both our pictures and we talked about our vacation for hours. Charlie thanked Joe for being on-call and asked him to come over for dinner because we were ordering in. Joe accepted. I think Joe liked Stephanie because he kept looking at her. Hmmm.. I thought he was with Julie. I asked Charlie and he told me they broke up. "Oh, I did NOT know that". I told Charlie that Steph told me she broke up with her boyfriend too but didn't tell me why. Charlie was talking with Joe about the job and what was going on and he told him what happened with our water problem. Joe said, "I thought it looked different in here. Holy Shit. That must have been horrible". Charlie told him how bad it was.

I gave Grams and Steph the trinkets I bought them on our trip. Grams liked snow globes, so I got her one of the colosseum in Rome. I got Steph a magnet for her fridge of the wine country and gave her a bottle of wine. Charlie picked up a token for Joe. I think he bought him a sweatshirt from Tuscany. We ordered food and we all had a nice dinner together. Steph stayed one more night. Charlie paid her and she left the next day.

16

SURPRISE BIRTHDAY GIFT

"Charlie?". He looked at me and said, "Uh oh, What?". I laughed. "I just wanted to ask you a question". He smiled at me and said, "I think I know what it is, but go ahead". I smiled back at him and said, "If you know what it is, then tell me how long". He came up to me and said, "Whenever you are ready, I am ready". I hugged him. "Really Charlie, really?" He said, "Yes, we are not getting any younger, let's do it". I was so happy. I told him that I really wanted to start a family and I wanted Grams to get to meet her great-grandchild. He said, "I would like that too Meggie. It's a special thing" And so it was!!! And we started trying. Day after day after day. It didn't take long and a month later I was pregnant. Charlie was so proud and he kept hugging and kissing me more than normal. We didn't say anything to Grams or anyone else until my first trimester was done. Grams was the first to know. Charlie and I went to the party store and found a tiny plastic baby doll and put a tissue diaper on it. We put it in a small box. We found out we were having a little girl a week later, so we put pink tissue paper on top of the baby doll, like a blanket and we wrapped up the box with birthday paper, because it just so happed that it was Grams birthday. Of course, we got her other stuff, but we wanted to give her this first. We took her out for dinner for her birthday to the Terrace View

Marina and Restaurant, where it all started with me and Charlie. Those electric kisses that go down to my toes are still there today. We had a small bag of gifts that Charlie hid in the trunk of the car. He had her arm and walked her to the door, while sneaky me got the bag out of the trunk and walked behind them. We had it all planned. We had reservations and Charlie asked the waiter to help us. They had pink roses on our table with pink napkins. Everything was pink at the table. He got her settled in her chair and I put the bag on the floor under my chair. We ordered a drink and some appetizers and while we waiting for them, Charlie winked at me. It was time to let her know. I took the bag out and handed it to Charlie. He took the little box out, all wrapped up in pink birthday paper. "Happy Birthday Grams. This is from the both of us". She had the biggest smile on her face. "Oh Thank you, you shouldn't have". We both busted out laughing and Charlie said, "I know, but we wanted to". She said, "What's so funny? Is this a gag gift?" We assured her it was not a gag gift. She tore open the birthday paper and looked at the box. Charlie said, "Good Things come in small boxes Grams". She opened the box, took out the pink paper and saw the baby doll. She opened her mouth wide in shock. "REALLY, REALLY? YOU ARE HAVING A BABY GIRL? IS THIS WHAT THIS MEANS?" She hugged us both and she was crying. Charlie gave her tissue and she kept crying. He leaned over and said, "I only have one more tissue" and she started laughing. "No wonder you were laughing. I get it now". She really was a pip. She opened her other gifts and they meant nothing after the first one. She said thank you for them, but all she cared about was the first one. She kept hugging me and then Charlie all through dinner. "I am so happy. Do you know how happy I am?" We told her we were happy too. We told her I was 3 months. I didn't have any morning sickness at all and my pregnancy was completely normal. I felt great. We had a wonderful dinner with Grams and after dinner we walked around the side of the restaurant to the lake so Grams could see the view. Charlie gave me an electric kiss and yes, I felt it down to my toes. We went home around 7:00 p.m. Grams had a permanent smile on her face. We invited Joe and Stephanie over for dinner the next night, so we could announce it. We told Grams and she said, "Oh those two are something else". I looked at Charlie and he said, "What do you mean Grams?" She said, "Oh you don't know? They have been smooching it up. Joe came over when you were in Italy". I smiled at Charlie, "I told you I saw him looking at her". Grams said, "Oh yeah, it's been going on for some time now, that is why he broke up with Julie". Charlie said, "WHAT? Really? Are you sure Grams?". She looked at Charlie, "Yes, I am sure. I have known this for a while. Steph told me and that is why she broke up with her boyfriend". Charlie and I looked at each other. I asked her, "Grams, did this happen when we were moving and packing?". She shook her head yes. All Charlie could say was, "Wow, ok". So now we invited both of them for dinner tomorrow night, so I am sure it's gonna come out. I told Charlie that I was gonna play a joke on them. I said, "I will say, if you tell me something, I will tell you something". He laughed. "Ok Meggie, that's a good way to tell them, but if they tell us before we ask? Then what?" I told him we would figure out a way.

The next morning, I put a pork loin roast in the crockpot with a bottle of Sweet Baby Rays BBQ sauce. I made some macaroni salad and a huge green bean salad. I took Grams and we went to the supermarket. I picked up some lettuce, pink napkins, sub rolls, and a cake mix with frosting and bouquet of pink roses. A strawberry cake mix with pink frosting of course. She picked up some snacks for herself while we were there. I picked up some appetizers and some pretzels. We went home and I made the cake. I decorated it with pink sprinkles and we put candles in it for Grams birthday because we didn't have a cake for her yet. I shredded the pork to make pulled pork and put it back in the crockpot. Everything was ready. Grams made a big salad. She used tomatoes and cucumbers from my garden. Grams insisted on setting the dining room table. We used the round kitchen table for the appetizers. Joe came first and he and Charlie were having a beer and talking out on the deck and then Steph showed up and we were talking in the kitchen. "Oooh, it smells good in here". I told her what we were having as I pulled some appetizers out of the oven. She tapped me on the arm. "I gotta tell you something Meg". I put the hot tray down on the pot holder and looked at her. "What's wrong?". She said, "Nothing is wrong. I just wanted to tell you that I am seeing Joe". I acted like it didn't know so Grams wouldn't get in trouble for telling. "What? You are? Umm. Isn't he seeing Julie?" She told me that he broke up with her and then started seeing her. "Oh, wow, This is exciting news Steph,

Congratulations". She said, "I have been seeing him for a while, but I didn't want to say anything until we knew it was serious". I said, "Oh, so I am guessing it's serious?". She blushed. "Yup, it is." I hugged her and told her I was happy for her. "Did you find a job yet, Steph". She said she had a promising interview with another medical center and she thinks she has it. She told me that she wouldn't have made it without us hiring her for Grams. I told her she would have. "You could have just come to me and I would have helped you out. You should know that Steph". She saw the cake on the counter and said, "Oh what a pretty cake. Is this for Grams birthday? I told her it was. Grams was sitting at the table and still had the same smile on her face as when we told her the news. Steph went to sit with her. "You are happy today Grams". Grams said, "Yes, it was my birthday yesterday and Charlie and Meegs took me out to dinner". I shook my head NO at her. I didn't think she would tell, and she didn't. She continued. "We didn't have a birthday cake, so I am having one today. Isn't it pretty?" Steph agreed. "Very pretty Grams". I put the roses on the table in between me and Charlie. I called Charlie and Joe to come in. Apparently, Joe told Charlie about him and Steph, when they were outside. They were talking about the tornado too. Everyone was picking on appetizers and Charlie made a couple of margaritas for us and they had beer. We all sat down for dinner and everyone was digging in. Charlie said, "Well, your secret is out of the bag and we have a secret too". Joe and Steph looked at each other and they knew. Steph said, "Pink Roses, pink napkins and a pink cake can only mean one thing. Are you pregnant with a little girl?" I shook my head yes. She started screaming. "OMG MEG, OMG MEG. THIS IS AWESOME NEWS, AWESOME. CONGRATULATIONS YOU GUYS". Joe shook Charlie's hand and got up to kiss me. "Wow you guys, this is the best news ever. Congratulations, wow" Grams started crying again and Charlie got up and handed her the box of Kleenex. She smiled at him. Steph looked at Grams, "What a wonderful birthday present you got. That is why you are so happy". Grams just started crying harder. Steph dried her tears. "Aww Grams, this is awesome".

We lit the candles and sang Happy Birthday to my Grams. Charlie handed her an envelope and said, "I sold your car Grams. Here ya go. We are not taking it. You have plenty of money to buy the baby clothes". She took the envelope and he wrote how much was in there. "You got that much? Ok, wow. I changed my mind. I am keeping it" And she started laughing. Steph asked when and I told her I was 3 months. We haven't picked a name yet, but we have plenty of time. My due date is March 10th.

We enjoyed the rest of the evening. We sat outside on the deck drinking margaritas and beer and we played cards. Grams excused herself around 9:30 and headed to bed. I asked if she wanted any help and she said no. I went with her anyway. I got her all tucked in bed, gave her a bottle of water, made her take her pill and put her TV on. I kissed her goodnight and she hugged me so tight.

I went back to our company. Steph and Joe were getting ready to leave and they were saying goodnight and they thanked us for dinner and for the good news. We congratulated them too. Charlie locked up and turned off the lights. He turned me towards him and gave me the biggest hug. He picked me up and said, "I have to do this while I still can" and he laughed and kissed me so long and my toes were tingling in mid air.

17

ELIZABETH LOUISE HUDSON

Charlie and I were thinking about names for our baby girl. We were going back and forth. We both made separate lists and then we put them together and crossed off certain names. We both liked Elizabeth, so that was going to be her first name. Charlie said we should give her Grams name as a middle name, so we decided her name would be Elizabeth Louise Hudson. It sounded regal and important, like an author. We would call her Liz or Lizzie. We weren't going to tell Grams yet, but we weren't going to wait too long to tell her. I loved the name so much, I started crying.

Charlie called his sister to tell her our news. "Ang?" She said, "Hi Char. How are things going with you guys". Charlie said, "I have news for you" and it got quiet. She said, "I am waiting, I am waiting". He said, "Meg and I are having a baby girl and she is due March 10th." Ang started screaming in the background for her husband Mike. "MIKE MY BROTHER IS GONNA BE A DADDY IN MARCH". Mike came to the phone and congratulated us. Angela was hysterical in the background. She finally came back to the phone and she was crying. "OH CHAR, THIS IS FANTASTIC NEWS. I AM SO HAPPY FOR YOU BOTH. What is her name going to be?" Charlie told her that her name was going to be Elizabeth Louise Hudson. Even

Angela said the name sounded important and she loved it. They talked for a while and they hung up.

I was 6 months now and I had 3 months to go. I had a belly now. Charlie would rub it every time he saw me. He would put his head on my belly and talk to Lizzie. My hormones were all over the place this past month. I cried about everything. I was so emotional over everything. I was looking at Facebook and some lady lost her dog and I bawled hysterically. Charlie knew what to expect I guess, because he was so supportive and comforting. He always made me feel better. He always dried my tears and said something to make me laugh and forget about what made me cry.

We decided to tell Grams what we picked for a name. She kept asking so Charlie said we would tell her at dinner tonight. He ordered Seafood from Dunbars Seafood and we ate Shrimp and lobster and clams. Grams enjoyed her seafood. I couldn't eat a lot of it now, but the doctor said once in a while was ok, so tonight was once in a while and I was loving it. Charlie asked Grams if she was enjoying it and she said she was. She was still sporting the smile that came with our news 3 months ago. It never left her face. I said, "So Grams, Charlie and I picked a name for the baby and we wanted to tell you tonight. Are you ready?" She said, "Of course I'm ready, as long as it's not one of those weird 'new' names like Sunshine or some shit like that". We started laughing and Charlie said, "It is going to be Elizabeth Louise Hudson. What do you think of that shit?" I started crying immediately because that is all I do lately.

Grams looked at us and said, "Are you kidding me? You are giving her my name?". Charlie said, "Is that ok Grams?" She smiled and said, "I am so fucking honored right now and your mom and dad are looking down on you right now Meegs, and they are the proudest parents in the whole wide world. I am so honored. Thank you both for this". And she started to cry. Charlie was prepared with the box of Kleenex for both of us. The smile on her face was priceless. It grew bigger from when she found out. She was so proud and she walked tall and smiled every minute of every day. She couldn't do enough for us. She kissed me and hugged me every chance she got and she caressed Charlie's arm when he was around her.

Charlie and I did some Christmas shopping for Grams and for his sister and brother-in-law. We asked Angela what the kids would like and if they made a list. She told me that Charlie always sent money. I told her that was not happening and that I wanted to buy something for them. She sent me a copy of their Christmas wishes list and Charlie and I went to town and bought them everything on the list. We wrapped everything up and found a box big enough to fit everything and Charlie took it to the post office and mailed it so it would get there for Christmas. I only bought for my Grams, because she was my only family and Steph. I splurged a bit for Steph because she was there for us, all year. No complaints at all. She just came and did whatever was necessary and we appreciated all of it. Charlie bought for Joe and his friends. Grams came with us to go shopping and she bought for her friends. She did the rest of her shopping on-line and we saw the packages piling up on the porch everyday.

Just before Christmas, a huge box was delivered by UPS. It was from Angela and Mike. I called Charlie to get it. He was out back in the yard, puttering around with the garden. He dragged it in and had a puzzled look on his face. "Should we open it now? Before Christmas?". I shook my head yes. The box was so big he couldn't lift it and had to drag it into the house. He said, "I don't think we should open it here in the entry way and I can't move it, unless I drag it. It was 4:00 p.m. He said, "I wonder if Joe is out of work yet? I will give him a call and see if he can help me. He called Joe and Joe was just leaving work and said he would be right over. The two of them pushed and pulled the box until they got it to the sitting room. Charlie took his knife and sliced open one side and Joe sliced open the other end of the box. They opened the box and inside was a white crib, a white dressing table, a white dresser, a crib mattress and a white padded rocking chair. It was the most beautiful baby furniture I ever saw. Charlie and I were supposed to go shopping for this stuff tomorrow. Joe helped him carry everything to the babies room. The crib had to be put together but I didn't want it done yet. Not until the baby was here. It is bad luck to do that. They set up the dresser and they put the changing table together and they put the rocking chair together. I just watched and cried. Joe kept looking at me and saying, "Are you alright?". Charlie assured him that I was and that I do a lot of crying these days. Charlie just said, "It's Hormones Joe". They finished and Charlie and Joe had a beer and Joe said he didn't mind taking the cardboard for him when he left. He picked up the cardboard and small box fell out. Charlie handed it to me and said, "Here babe, open this one and he sliced it open for me". I opened the box and it was a wooden plaque for a door and it said, "Lizzie Hudson". It was pink with white writing. AND, I started crying. I told Charlie not to put it up yet. We called Angela and Mike that night to thank them for such a generous gift. They were worried that we already bought it and we told them we were going tomorrow, so it got here right on time. I started crying and Angela said, "Oh hon you are so ready, if your hormones are that bad. I couldn't thank her enough and Charlie was so overwhelmed he was tearing up, but quickly wiped the tears away. He thanked them both for what they did.

We had Steph and Joe over for Christmas Eve because they were busy on Christmas Day. We had drinks and appetizers and we exchanged gifts. I showed Steph the room with all the new furniture that Charlie's family sent.

Christmas Day was just our regular dinner party. Charlie, me and Grams and that was fine with me. I was getting tired. I was taking naps during the day. I wasn't interested in going out for dinner. We did the same for New Year's Eve and Day and before you know it, it was Valentine's Day.

I was 8 months now and I was as big as a house and I didn't want to move. Charlie insisted on taking me and Grams out for dinner. I think he missed going out, so I went. He had flowers for both of us and he bought me a huge heart of chocolate. Yeah, just what I needed, more fat to weigh me down. I was starting to feel sorry for myself and fat. I was feeling fucking fat and I was. We did have a nice time when we went out for dinner though and I was in a much better mood when we got home. I had one month to go.

18

WELCOME LITTLE ONE

The baby was kicking more and more every day and sometimes she was really hurt me. She would kick me under my ribs and I would lose my breath and the doctor said she was in position and that was perfectly normal.

We were down to the wire. Charlie and I shopped for diapers and onesies and nightgowns and little hats and booties and mittens. We bought a couple of blankets, bottles, binkies and receiving blankets. He bought a diaper genie and refill bags and a monitor. I had no idea what we needed, so we tried to get a little of everything. I know my Grams probably had a truck load of stuff coming.

I wasn't due till the 10th and it was March 2. Charlie was making me some breakfast and Grams came in to eat and patted me on the back. "How's it going Mama?" I told her I felt like I was going to explode. I was miserable and fat. I ate breakfast and got up to go to the bathroom and my water broke all over the dining room floor. Charlie just looked at me and I looked at him and he had his mouth open. "UM, What do I do now?". I laughed at him. "You are gonna get my bag and put it in the car and we will wait till my contractions start and see how far apart they are and you will call the doctor and tell him my water broke". We were 20 minutes from the hospital. He dropped the dish on the floor, but it fell on the rug and didn't break. "Uh ok. I am so nervous". I looked at him and said, "YOU?, you are nervous. Look at me Charlie". He said, "Ok, I will have to take charge here, I guess" and he started laughing. "I am kidding with you babe. I know what to do. Do you have any contractions yet?" I told him not yet, but as I was saying it, one started. It was a strong one, or so I thought. I needed to sit down, but I was all wet. He took me to the bedroom and helped me change and he washed my legs down and dried me off. He put a pair of prego leggings on me and gave me my hoodie. He got on the phone to the doctor's office to let them know my water broke. They said they would give the doctor the message and I should come to the hospital when my contractions were 5 minutes apart. He got me comfortable in bed and Grams came in and sat with me while he cleaned up the kitchen. Charlie called Steph to let her know and Steph offered to come and stay with Grams while I was in the hospital and Charlie thanked her for that. "I will be right there. I just have to pack a few things". My contractions were 15 minutes apart, so it would be a while before Lizzie arrived. Steph came and she settled in the spare room and Grams went to her room. Steph came in and she was timing the contractions until Charlie was able to come and do it. They were steady at 15 minutes apart. They were about the same strength as the first one. Charlie finally came in and said my bag was in the car and so was his. He said he was staying with me. He told me he called the doctors office and they were aware and that we would leave when they were 5 minutes apart. Just rest Meggie. It's gonna be awhile before we go anywhere. I said, "What took you so long. What were you doing?". He told me he had to clean up the water breakage. "OH, I forgot about that. Sorry". He looked at me and said, "For real? You are gonna apologize for that? I love you Meggie. More than you will ever know. I was in labor all day and the contractions were now 10 minutes apart. It was 8:00 p.m. I was hungry, but Charlie said that if I ate, I might get sick when I got a contraction and that the doctor told him not to give me anything but ice chips, and water or jello. "Do you want some Jello Meggie?" I told him I wanted a fucking hamburger and he laughed at me. "Sorry, no can do. After you have the baby, we will have BBQ hamburgers on the grill. OK?" Another hour went by and they were down to 8 minutes apart and they were getting stronger. Grams came in and said, "Keep a close eye on her because they could all of a sudden get real close" and she left. Another hour went by and they were 6 minutes apart and I was starting to scream a little with the contractions. They were getting bad. I saw Charlie getting nervous. "Do you want to go now? Maybe by the time we get you out to the car, they could be 5?" I said, "Let's go. Charlie. I don't think it's gonna be too much longer". Charlie let Grams know we were leaving and that Steph would be here for her. Charlie got me to the car and we took off for the hospital. I got 4 contractions in those 20 minutes, which means they were 5 minutes apart. It was 10:30 p.m. and I was in so much pain. I was getting dry heaves with the contractions and spitting up water. Charlie gave me paper towels. He pulled up to the emergency room entrance and he had called ahead. They came out with a wheelchair. He pulled the car up and parked in one of the spaces available. He ran in to catch up with me. They brought me straight up to the maternity ward. The nurse got me undressed and into a gown. They examined me and now the contractions were 4 minutes apart. I was 8 centimeters dilated. She told me it would be another hour or two. Charlie held my hand the whole time and he kissed my forehead and gave me ice chips. "You are doing good Meggie. I love you babe". He told me this for another 1 1/2 hours. It was just after midnight, about 12:10 a.m. and they were coming fast and I was screaming with pain and there were a bunch of nurses in there and the doctor came in. "Push Meg, Push." I had a nurse holding one hand and Charlie holding the other. I had a nurse putting cold compresses on my forehead because I was sweating so bad, and the doctor looking up my hoo ha saying push, push. I just wanted to scream at everyone to get the hell out and leave me alone. I was tired. "I can't do this, I can't". I heard Charlie's voice. "Come on Meggie, you can do it. Lizzie needs you to push". I heard that and when the next contraction came, I heard the doctor say push Meg and I did. Elizabeth Louise Hudson was born at 12:18 a.m. on 03/03/20. Look at that fucking number, will you? Look at it. Don't tell me numbers don't mean a thing because they do. She came out screaming and Charlie cut the cord and he was crying the whole time. They put her on my chest and he was kissing me. "Look Babe, she is fucking gorgeous. She is the most beautiful baby ever". The nurse even said. "She is a pretty baby". She had a full head of black hair. She weighed in at 8 lbs 10 oz and she was 19 inches long. Charlie took our picture together and sent it to Grams, Steph, Joe and his sister and the text read, "Meet Miss Elizabeth Louise Hudson. She was born at 12:18 a.m. on 3/03/20. She weighs 8 lbs 10 oz and she is 19 inches long" He took a selfie with all 3 of us and kept sending all the pictures to everyone. They cleaned her up and wrapped her in a receiving blanket and she had a pink hat on. They handed her to Charlie and he was sobbing. The nurse took a few pictures of him holding Lizzie with his phone and I sent them and thanked the nurse. They cleaned me up and I was so exhausted, but I wanted to hold her one more time before they took her. The nurse let me hold her for about 5 minutes. She said she would bring her back in the morning and she wanted me to get some rest. They had a bed in the room for Charlie. He was laying next to me in my bed and kissing me. "Charlie?". "What babe?". I said, "She was born on 3/03/20. Do you believe the numbers now?" He just looked at me and said, "OMG, are you kidding me?. Yes, yes, I believe in the numbers now. I DO, I do". And he did believe in the numbers from this day forward. He said, "Meggie, Thank you for today. You gave me the most beautiful daughter. I knew you would be the best thing that ever happened to me when I saw you in my backyard." I hugged him and said, "Charlie, you are the best thing that ever happened to me too. I could not ever ask for a better friend, lover or companion. I love you so much". I guess he held me until I fell asleep and then he got in the other bed.

I woke up to my little Lizzie crying. The nurse got me up to go to the bathroom and get cleaned up. Charlie was holding the baby and they were waiting for me to breast feed. We decided to do that for the first month and then we would go to formula, that is unless she wouldn't take my breast. I came out and they put me in a chair and Charlie handed me Lizzie. I was staring at her and tearing up. She really was a beautiful baby. The nurse showed me how to hold her and breastfeed. She latched right on and the nurse said my milk came in. I knew it did, because I was so sore and swollen. She stopped feeding and she was content and she opened her eyes and looked at me. "Hi Lizzie, I love you" She blinked at me. I kept talking to her and Charlie was leaning over and he was talking to her too. She was very alert and was listening to us. She was awake for quite a while and we took turns holding her and talking to her. Then Charlie was rocking her and she fell asleep, so he put her back in the basinet. The nurse came in and said we were going home tomorrow. Two days and you are out. I didn't care because I knew I would be much more comfortable at home. Charlie said that Joe came and put the crib together and put a sheet on the mattress and we were all set. We had a surprise visitor that afternoon. Steph brought Grams to see Miss Elizabeth. I thought she was smiling before? Oh her smile was priceless as she sat in the chair and Charlie handed her Elizabeth Louise Hudson. She started crying and was so happy. Steph asked me how I was and I told her fine, just sore and tired. Steph said she would stay for a while till we got on our feet and she said she didn't mind at all. (Charlie paid her anyway).   Steph handed me a white bag and had one for Charlie too. I smelled food. Charlie gave her a huge hug. I am starving. Thank you for this. She got him 2 big macs, French fries and handed him a chocolate shake. I had a one big mac, French fries and a vanilla shake. I said, "You are a god send. I love you". I really wanted a big hamburger when I started labor, but I couldn't eat. Charlie was stuffing himself and so was I and Grams just sat in that chair loving on her Great Granddaughter. Lizzie was awake for most of Grams visit and Grams talked to her the whole time. Charlie took a lot of pictures of her holding the baby. He sent the pics to his sister. Ang wrote back and said, "That is Meg's grandma, right?". Charlie told her yes and her name was Louise Farigno. Ang said, "Oh, ok, so that's where Louise came from. That is so precious that Meg did that, Char. You landed a sweetheart. I hope you know that". Charlie told her that we both decided on giving her that name. He said, "Does that mean I am a sweetheart too?" And he laughed. Ang said, "You have always been a sweetheart to me Char and you always will be". He told Ang that he knows I am a sweetheart and that I am the best thing that ever happened to him. Steph told Grams it was time to go and there was a little bit of resistance. She didn't want to leave, but Charlie told her we were coming home tomorrow afternoon and she could hold her as long as she wanted. She smiled at him and said, "Promise?" Charlie promised her. She finally left willingly. She will do anything Charlie asks of her. She listens better to him than she does anyone. She kissed me before she left and told me that Lizzie was beautiful. "I can't wait till you guys get home". I told her I would be home before she knew it.

Charlie and I were ready to go. He brought the carseat up from the car and we got her all dressed in her new outfit and put a bow in her hair to match. He took a picture and sent it to Steph and Grams and said, "I am on my way home". I had black stretch pants on and thank god they fit. I was still very swollen and my stomach was huge. The nurse told me that the longer I breast feed, the faster it will go down. I said, "Really?". She smiled and "Yup, keep breastfeeding and you will be back to normal before you know it". I decided that's what I would do and then go to formula.   I sat in the backseat with Lizzie on the way home. We got home and there were a bunch of cars in the driveway. We pulled into the garage and Charlie helped me out and then grabbed the baby and we walked up to the walkway into the house. "SURPRISE, SURPRISE". OMG. It was a small baby shower given by Steph, Joe and Grams. My boss and a couple of my friends from work, Charlie's sister came with Mike and the kids, his aunt and uncle, and Charlie's friends from work. They catered food and the whole house was decorated with pink balloons and pink table cloths and napkins and pink roses. It was absolutely beautiful. There was folding table on one side of my living room with a pink table cloth draped over it and it was full of gifts for Lizzie. There was a cute cake with baby bottles and a baby on it and it said, "Welcome, Elizabeth Louise Hudson". It had pink roses all around it. I looked at Charlie, "Did you know about this?" He swore he didn't know anything. Lizzie was sleeping, but Grams wanted to hold her, so Steph helped her into the recliner and Charlie, as promised, let her hold her. We went around kissing and hugging everyone and thanking them for coming. I was tired and I told Charlie I needed to sit down. He got me comfortable in my recliner and then got me some food. There was soft music playing from somewhere. Probably from someone's phone. Everyone ate and Steph and Joe had a pot of coffee on. Steph and Charlie waited on me. I was really sore and still tired and Grams was still holding Lizzie an hour later. Even though she was sleeping, Grams continued to talk to her. Everyone was taking pictures of them. Charlie told Grams that he wanted to put the baby in the basinet and that she had to eat something. She agreed. He had the basinet in the sitting room and everyone would walk by and peek at her. But the party was in the dining room and living room. It was still noisy, but she slept through it, which is awesome. Charlie asked Grams what she wanted to eat and got it for her. We all had cake and coffee and then they wanted me to open all the gifts. I got so many nice things for her. I got a stroller with a mosquito netting and a little pool. We got another monitor and bibs, teethers, bottles, binkies, drawstring nightgowns, diapers (tons of diapers) and onesies and cute little dresses with bows for her hair and a sound machine and stuffed animals, blankets and toddler toys. We got sheets for the crib and for the changing table. There was so much stuff. Charlie was helping me open the gifts because there were so many. I looked at Grams and I think her smile was permanent. She looked at me with so much love in her eyes and she kept looking at Charlie the same way. Steph and Joe started cleaning up. Joe went around to everyone with a trash bag and everyone just threw their plates, cups and napkins in it. They had dixie cups for the coffee so everything was disposable. It was smart thinking on their part. Grams and Joe paid for the shower and all the food and Steph paid for all the paper goods, and balloons.   Charlie kept patting Joe on the back and thanking him for all of it. Steph was waiting on me hand and foot and I thanked her for everything. "What would I do without you Steph. You are the best friend I ever had". She smiled at me and said, " I am here for as long as you need me". I told her she would be sorry for that statement. She just laughed. Steph said Ang and Mike and the kids were all set up in the spare rooms. Charlie's aunt and uncle went home. She took one of the attic rooms so the kids could have her room. She told me she set up the air mattresses and Ang helped her. The babies room wasn't being used yet and the basinet would be in our room. She told me not to worry about anything, so I didn't. I must of dozed off for a while because when I woke up, I was still in the recliner and no one was around, except Charlie, who was sitting on the couch watching me. "Good Morning". That startled me. "Morning?" He laughed and said, "I'm kidding. You slept for an hour. Your body needs it". I looked around and he had moved the basinet into the living room near me and I saw Lizzie's pretty face. She was still sleeping, but she was making stretchy noises and I knew it was almost time for her to eat. Charlie got me set up and got a cloth diaper to put over me. We waited until she fully woke up and started crying slightly. He picked her up and hugged her and handed her to me. She latched on to me right away and she was feeding. Charlie just sat back and was smiling. "You are a good mommy, Meggie, just like I knew you would be". When she was done, I burped her and then held her and talked to her and rocked her. She was blinking at me and making little noises. She smiled at me and then farted. Charlie burst out laughing. I told him it was a fake smile. They always do that when they pass gas. He said, "Maybe it wasn't gas. Give her to me and I will change her. She has to be soaked". He went to change her and brought her back. He was laughing. "Yup, she was soaked and it wasn't a fart. I changed her and then she shit in the new diaper, so I let her finish and now we are on diaper number 2". I started laughing. "She is a poopy little girl". He looked at me and said, "You look so tired Meggie. Why don't you go get comfy and get into bed? I will help you with the baby". He put the baby in her basinet and gave me his hand and lifted me out of the chair. I walked down to the bedroom and changed into sweats, used the bathroom and got into bed. I think my head hit the pillow and I was out. I didn't sleep well in the hospital. The bed was so uncomfortable. They had me propped up and I can't sleep like that. Every time I put the bed down, a nurse would come in and prop me up again. I couldn't wait to get home so I could sleep flat and on my side. I though I heard Lizzie crying and woke up. Charlie was in bed and sleeping too. I must have been dreaming because I looked over and she was sound asleep. I went back to sleep. A couple hours later, she woke up for a feeding and Charlie got her for me and I fed her, burped her and talked to her and rocked her. He took her and changed her for me again. I said, "What would I do without you Charlie Hudson?" He just smiled at me. "She is mine too and we have to share responsibility. It's not just your job ya know?"

I had no idea what time it was. Charlie said it was 2:00 a.m. I told him we had to keep track of the times and the feedings. He got his notebook out of his night table and wrote down that we fed her at 2:00 a.m. He said, "Her last feeding was at 10:00, so she went 4 hours. That's good for a newborn right?" I told him it was normal. I told him that we would have to sleep when she was sleeping, so we could keep up with her. We both laid down and went back to sleep. I heard her crying and Charlie said it was 6:15 a.m. She was right on time. He got up and handed her to me and I fed her and burped her and he changed her diaper and she was just making little noises in her basinet. Steph stayed with us for a month. She was such a big help. She did some cooking and did laundry and helped with Grams and with me and with the baby. Charlie paid her very well before she left.

19

NEW ADDITION?

As time went by, Lizzie started sleeping longer between feedings. We were up to 6 hours when she was 2 months old, which was good because I would feed her at 9:00 p.m. and we only had to get up once during the night at about 3-3:30. Then she would sleep till about 9:00 a.m. I usually got up before that and pumped some milk. I was trying to get enough so she could start taking the bottle and that way Grams or Charlie could feed her. And, I would know how much she was getting. Charlie started calling me a cow, because I had so much milk. The fridge was full of bottles so we decided to freeze some. I was almost done breast feeding. I lost all my weight and I looked pretty good for giving birth 3 months ago. So, I stopped when she was 3 1/2 months. Grams got to feed her the bottle and she was so happy. Lizzie was drinking 8 oz at a feeding, but also going longer between feedings. We started giving her cereal and then fruit. She was growing fast. She was starting to make noises and trying to talk and she was laughing. This is such a fun age. Charlie and Grams were having a blast with her. I had to fight to get some time with her. Every time, she would laugh or try to talk, they both laughed. I am so happy that my Grams got to see her Great Granddaughter. It meant so much to me. It was like her reward for taking care of me all my life.

Charlie kept his promise to her about holding the baby for as long as she wanted. She kept telling him. "Charlie, you are good man. I love you". He smiled at her every time and said, "I love you too Grams"..

Lizzie was getting big and the doctor said she was in the 75th percentile in her growth chart. She was a healthy little girl. For those of you that want to know what she said first.... It was Da Da. Then came Ma Ma. And then the day came when she said GAM. It wasn't really clear, but she said it and she only said it when she saw her GAM. The look on my Grams face was so priceless. She said, "Did you hear her Meegs? I think she said my name. I think she said GAM. Did you hear her?" I told her I did and Lizzie was smiling at her and she kept saying it. I think Lizzie knew how important that was. She was too heavy for Grams now, but she sat in her highchair and Grams played with her and talked to her all day long. She kept her busy with toys and talking while I was busy getting dinner or doing laundry. Charlie built another garden box for the plants in the yard. We decided that it was better out in the yard than on the deck. The animals couldn't get into it and the wire protected it from the wind. He built 2 small ones instead of 1 big one. Joe came to help him move them from the garage out to the backyard. They stapled the wire onto the posts and he put the doors on and then they dug up the grass and they planted the cucumbers, the tomatoes and peppers and all the stuff that we usually had in pots on the deck. Joe took a few pots for his yard because we didn't need them all now. I started seedlings in them in the garage under a grow light and then Charlie would plant them when they were ready. We had a system and it was working. He loved working in the garden and always had a big smile on his face when he picked the veggies and brought them up to me for cooking. He was so proud of them. I knew the feeling because I had it when I lived behind him. I swear to God. There wasn't one weed in those garden boxes. Not one! I remember laughing when he lived behind me and he would be pulling weeds and I was saying to myself. I bet there are no weeds in his grass. I was probably right. We had squash, cucumbers, 4 different kinds of tomatoes, spaghetti squash, different kinds and colors of peppers, watermelon, basil and parsley. Grams loved the stuffed cubanelles and so did Charlie. I usually cleaned and cut the other peppers into strips and froze them for recipes. I always dried the basil and parsley at the end of their growing season and then we started all over with new plants. The cucumbers were abundant and we alway had enough to share with Joe and Steph. The watermelons were almost ready and those were my favorite and I couldn't wait to give Lizzie some to try. I roasted the cherry tomatoes with garlic and olive oil in my air fryer and we had bruschetta. If we had a lot of tomatoes, I made sauce with them. We also had a lot of loaded tomato salads during the summer months. I also got an awesome recipe to make bread, so I was busy doing that once a week. I made pizza dough, rolls and bread. We were never short on that stuff.

Lizzie was a year old now and she was such a good baby. She was saying please and thank you and she was calling Grams, Gamma and that made her so happy. She was picking up a lot of words and starting to form little sentences. Oh and she loved watermelon like her mommy. She was brought up on all the garden stuff so she loved it. We weren't big on giving her sugar and we didn't eat much of it either, but for a birthday, we would have cake and I made her cookies once in a while, but those were treats. Charlie tried his hand at Green Leaf lettuce and it was a success, so I wouldn't have to buy that anymore. We had it coming out of our ears and we shared with Steph and Joe. We ate lettuce every single day. Lizzie liked it too but she liked the oil and balsamic vinegar dressing on it or she wouldn't eat it. She was only eating our food now. No baby food and I would give her blueberries, blackberries, raspberries and strawberries. Those were her favorites.

One night after Lizzie's First Birthday, I decided it was time to talk about having another baby. Charlie knew it was coming. All I had to say was, "Charlie?" In a certain voice and he knew. "Sure I am ready when you are". And so it was…. We started trying and as usual, it didn't take long. One and half months later I told Charlie I was pregnant by putting a T-Shirt on Lizzie that said, "Big Sister to be". He came in from the backyard and saw it. He ran to me and picked me up and kissed me and hugged me. "This is fucking fantastic. I am so excited. See if you can conjure up a little boy in there". I laughed and said, "Will you be disappointed if it's not?" He said, "Absolutely not, we will just try till I get one". He laughed and I laughed and said, "UM, no". He said, "What do you mean no?" I said, "I mean no, we are not gonna keep trying till we get a boy because we may end up with 10 kids" and I just laughed.

He said, "Oh I wouldn't go that far. Maybe 9 though".
Then he said he was just kidding. I told him it was him that
decided whether it was a boy or girl and this was news to
him. "You can't blame this on me" and he was on his
phone googling what I just told him. He raised his
eyebrows and said, "Wow, I never knew that". And I quote,
"A child's biological sex (male or female) is determined by
the chromosome that the male parent contributes". I told
him that I have XX chromosomes and he has X and Y and
whatever matches up with my X chromosome determines
whether it is a male of female. "You gave an X last time. If
you gave a Y this time, then it is a boy." He smiled at me
and said, "Whatever it is I will be happy. You know that".
We left the T-shirt on Lizzie so Grams would see it at dinner
time, but Grams came out of her room early and started to
play with Lizzie in her high chair. She didn't even pay
attention to what she was wearing until about an hour later
when I pulled Lizzie out of her high chair to change her and
I stood her up in front of Grams. She saw it and she
opened her mouth wide, "OMG, YOU ARE GONNA HAVE
ANOTHER BABY MEEGS?" I shook my head and gave her
a hug with Lizzie. She asked me if it was a surprise and I
told her that it was planned. She said, "OOOOHH I hope
it's a boy, Please God, let it be a boy". I told her Charlie
was praying for a boy too and told her our conversation.
She laughed and said, "He can't blame you". I told her I
wasn't sure how far a long I was. We have been trying for 6
weeks and I took a test this morning and it's positive. I
haven't tested in 3 weeks though, so I don't know. I told
her and Charlie at dinner that I have a doctor's appointment

next week. Charlie was feeding Lizzie some squash that I simmered with salt and pepper and onion and garlic powder and she was loving it. "MORE". He was telling her "Ok, chew that".

We went to the appointment today and my doctor said I was 2 months, but I didn't believe him. "How can that be? Maybe 1 month, but not 2." I told him we tried for 6 weeks, so I can't be 2 months. He suggested an ultrasound and he scheduled it for next week. Steph came to babysit for Lizzie and stayed with Grams and Charlie and I went to the ultrasound. I was ready and we were both waiting for the nurse to come in. She started looking around. "Hmm." She said that 2 more times and then Charlie finally said, "Um, can you tell us what's going on?". She said, "I'm sorry, I don't see a fetus. Let me go get the doctor". I started crying immediately. "OMG Charlie, what's going on?" The doctor came in and took over the ultrasound. He moved it down further than my uterus. "Ah ha. I see the problem. You are definitely pregnant Meg, but the baby is not in the uterus. It is attached to the outside wall of the uterus. I'm sorry, but we have to remove it." Me and Charlie started crying. Charlie asked him how dangerous it was and if I could still have children after that. The doctor assured him that it happens all the time. "It's not dangerous. I can do it right here and Meg can still have children. Let's take care of this now, ok? If I don't, you will start having excruciating pain as the baby grows and that will be dangerous. Sorry guys, I am really sorry". They prepped me and he took care of it right in the office. We left an hour later and Charlie and I were so sad and I was sobbing in the car. He was staying strong for me, but I know he crying inside. We didn't say anything to anyone when we got home. Charlie went out to the garden, where I am sure he was crying his heart out, and I went into my room. Steph knew something was wrong. She knocked on my door and came in and I was balling my eyes out. "OMG. What happened honey? What's wrong?" I told her and she started crying with me. She told me it's gonna be ok. You can have another one. This one just wasn't meant to be. I told her, "I can't tell my Grams, I just can't". She told me that she would tell her. Steph called Joe for Charlie and he came running over and went out back. I looked out to check on Charlie and saw him with his head on Joe's shoulder. Joe was holding him and trying to console him. He was crying so hard and then I cried even harder after seeing this.   I told Steph "I need my Lizzie". She brought Lizzie to me but she had taken the T-shirt off her and I laid on the bed with her crying. Lizzie knew I was sad and kept saying "Mommie, Mommie". Joe came in with Charlie and they were having a shot and a beer and Joe calmed him down. Steph went out to them and told them I was in the bedroom with Lizzie crying. Charlie came in and said, "Come on Babe, We need to calm down. I know this is sad and believe me, I just cried my eyes out, but we need to put this behind us and start over. We can try again ok?" He dried my tears and he took Lizzie with him and gave me his hand and pulled me up. "Come on Meggie. We can do this. At least months didn't go by. It's only been a week. Let's be strong together babe". I got up. Grams met us in the hallway and she kissed me. "It's gonna be ok, sweetheart. You can try again. It just wasn't meant to be. Your mom lost one too, before you". I looked at her. "You never told me that Grams. Did she lose any after me?" She shook her head no. We all went to the kitchen where Joe and Steph were and we all had a drink. I didn't want a Margarita. I wanted a shot of whiskey, a couple shots of whiskey, I wanted to get drunk, but I couldn't because of Lizzie. I did have 3 shots though and I was feeling woozy, but I felt better about the whole thing. Everyone was so positive and telling us we could try again and it would be fine. It was just a fluke. Joe said, "It happens a lot and it's good that you found out so early. Can you Imagine if you waited 4 months and then had the ultrasound, which is normally when that is done? That would be devastating, but Megs, it's only been a week. It doesn't make it better, but it does, you know what I mean?" I shook my head. I understood what he said. He said, "I am so sorry you guys, but I know you will be calling us in a couple months telling us you are pregnant. I know it". I kissed him on he cheek. "Thanks Joe. You made me feel better." Charlie kissed me. "Look at all the fun we will have trying for that baby". I kissed him and smiled. "Yup". Grams didn't say a word the whole time. I knew she was sad for us. She didn't have to say anything. Lizzie saw all the kissing going on and kissed her Daddy and then she wanted to come to me. I grabbed her and she kissed me too.

The doctor recommended that we wait two months before trying again. So I went back on my birth control and we waited. Charlie was so loving and understanding through those 2 months. He knew I was still sad and he tried to keep me positive and smiling. "Look at this beautiful little girl we have. She makes me smile and laugh all day everyday." He tried so hard and he did make me smile and laugh, but I wanted another child so bad. I was trying to stay positive. Finally our two months was up and I stopped the birth control and we had a lot of fun trying for our baby. Two months went by and nothing. I saw the doctor and he assured me there was nothing wrong. "Keep trying hon, it will happen." I smiled and we left the office.

Charlie had the radio on in the car and he started singing the song that was playing. He was so fucking funny, I became hysterical laughing. He did it. He made me laugh and forget. He said, "What do you say that we go in the pool when we get home. We can put Lizzie in the playpen and go in." I said, "It sounds like a plan. I am in". Steph called me on the way home and asked how things were and I told her the story. "Can I come over for a while to see Lizzie?". I said, "Sure. Everything ok Steph?" She said, "Yes and No". I told Charlie. He said, "Joe told me they had a fight last week and they weren't speaking to one another". I said, "Oh God, no, I hope they make up soon. That is devastating." Steph was there when we got home. She was sitting in the driveway with her car. She got out when we pulled in. Charlie took Lizzie out of the backseat and I got out. "What's going on Steph?". She said, "Joe is mad at me. I tried to explain but he won't even listen to me". I asked what happened. She said she went to Starbucks to get a coffee and saw a guy that she knew from high school and he hugged her and it just so happened that Joe was walking in to get a coffee too. He became jealous and she couldn't even introduce him. He left and he wouldn't even listen to her. "So if he won't listen to me, how can I can tell him he is just a friend, how am I gonna settle this with him?" Charlie heard her side of the story and said, "I usually don't like to get involved with other people's problems, but I can say something to Joe that he needs to listen to your side of the story. I won't say anything other than that Steph. Just that he needs to listen to you ok?" She agreed and thanked him. I said, "Well now that you are here, wanna watch Lizzie so we can go swimming? We are gonna put her in the playpen out on the deck". She said she would love to. Charlie told her we were ordering take out and she could stay if she wanted. "We are getting Chinese. Miss Lizzie likes the Lo Mein". Steph laughed. She didn't ask me anything about being pregnant and I was happy about that because I didn't want to think about it anymore. Charlie said we should just take it easy and if it happens, it happens and we both just need to stay calm and relax. He said that's when it happens. So I am taking his advice. I told Charlie that when I become pregnant, we weren't telling anyone until my first trimester was over and we know everything is ok and he agreed.

So we kept trying but at a relaxed pace, every day until it finally happened.   It took another month before it happened. The doctor did another ultrasound to make sure the baby was inside the uterus, per our request. And it was fine. We waited until we found out if it was a boy or a girl first before we told anyone. I was showing, and I think my Grams knew, but she never said a word. I was 4 months and we went to the ultrasound and Charlie was so excited.

He wanted a boy in the worst way. If this was a boy, we both agreed that this would be it for our family. If it was another girl, we would try one more time for a boy. I got the gown on and I was laying on the table and we were waiting for the sonographer to come in. Charlie was holding my hand and kissing my face. She saw how excited we were and said, "So I am assuming you want to know the sex of the baby?" Charlie said, "Yes, yes, we want to know". She was the same woman who did my last one. "Congratulations you guys. I am happy for you". She put the jelly on and started looking. "Meg, are you taking fertility drugs?". I told her I wasn't and asked why she asked me that. She got up and said, "I'll be right back". The doctor came in and I was already crying. "Aw. Meg, everything is fine. Don't cry". He put it back on my belly and said, "Look Guys, Look here and here. You are having twins. Looks like identical twins, both boys. See this right here and here? Two winky dinks." And he started laughing. Charlie turned white. I didn't and couldn't even talk. Charlie said, "TWINS? BOYS?" The doctor told him it was true. He gave us a few pictures to take home. On one of them, he circled the winky dinks and made a smily face on it. I loved this doctor. He was funny and he was serious. He was very caring and thoughtful and considerate. He was honest and sincere. I looked at Charlie and tears were streaming down his face. "Thank you Meggie, Thank you Babe. I love you so much". I said, "Remember what I told you about the chromosomes? It was you that decided what we are having, not me". The doctor said, "She is right Charlie. It was all you, but it is her that decided you were having twins and it was her that decided if they were identical or not." He looked at me, "Now Meg. Having twins, is not like the pregnancy you had with Lizzie. You will be carrying a lot of weight and you are little, so I want you to be very careful, walking and going up and downstairs. I want to see you in here every month and if you are concerned about anything, I want to see you. You probably won't go full term so when you are nearing the end of your 7th month, we will need you to come in once a week. I want to give you some prenatal vitamins that are by prescription only, because these boys will take everything you have, vitamin wise and you will need to supplement that. Anything out of the ordinary, I want you to call. I am giving you my cell number in case you need to reach me on the weekend or after hours. I want to know everything ok?" He handed his number to Charlie. Charlie shook his hand and he still had tears coming down his face. The doctor said, "Are those scared tears or tears of happiness?" He laughed and Charlie told him happiness tears. I got dressed and Charlie got another appointment for next month. We walked out holding hands and the staff was congratulating us. They were all smiling at us. He kissed me all the way to the car and in the car. "Charlie?". He said, "Yes my love?". I said, "Can we go to the mall and get a T-Shirt for Lizzie?" He laughed. "Um, no, we are not doing that this time". I said, "Ok, what are we doing?" He said, "Remember how we told Grams about Lizzie?". I smiled and said, "Yes, ok, Let's buy two tiny babies and wrap them in blue diapers". He said, "Yup, that's what I was thinking and is it possible to get blue roses?" I told him it was. He said, "Lets invite Joe and Steph for dinner. We will get Mexican if you want or Chinese. Up to you". I said I would rather have Chinese and Lizzie liked Lo Mein. He said, "Ok, then we will get two bouquets of blue roses and the 2 babies in a box with blue tissue paper." We stopped at the florist and got 2 bouquets of blue roses and went to the party store and got 2 of the tiny babies and some blue tissue paper. Lizzie was looking at all the stuff in the party store and kept reaching for things. Charlie gave her a toy from the shelf and he bought it for her. I did the wrapping in the car. We bought white wrapping paper. We bought a blue paper table cloth and blue napkins. I sent a text to Steph and Joe and invited them to dinner from Charlie's phone. I just put, "Chinese Food. Our House. Five o"Clock". We parked in the driveway and Charlie ordered the Chinese Food through Door Dash and then he got Lizzie out and I got out with my shopping bags. Grams had no idea where we went. We just told her we were going out and asked if she needed anything. We walked into the house and she came out of her room. "Where did you guys go?" I told her we went to do some shopping. "We are having Chinese food tonight Grams, Ok?" She smiled and said ok and she was talking to Lizzie. Charlie put her in the playpen and Grams instantly sat down next to her and was playing and talking to her. I was smiling from ear to ear and Charlie was too. I think she knew, but she didn't know everything. I hope she doesn't have a heart attack. Charlie heard back from Joe and Steph and they were coming and Joe said he made up with Steph. He took Charlie's advice and listened to her.

Steph and Joe came in one car and the food came right after they arrived. I had the dining room all set up with the flowers, tablecloth and napkins. You can't see the dining room from the front door. You actually have to go through the kitchen and go around the corner, so grams couldn't even see it from where she was with Lizzie. Charlie walked in as I was putting the roses on the table. He grabbed me and kissed me and picked me up. "I love you Meg Hudson. You still do things to me when I look at you". I hugged him tight and said, "Enjoy this while you can because I will be a blimp very soon". He laughed and said, "I will still love you as a blimp". The doorbell rang. Charlie went to get it and the food and Steph and Joe were there. He grabbed the food, tipped the guy and Steph and Joe came in. Joe smiled at him. "Do you have good news for us? Is this why the dinner party?" Charlie said, "I have no idea what you are talking about". He left them and they followed him to the kitchen. Charlie said, "Ok Food is here and he grabbed Lizzie and put her in her highchair and gave her the toy he bought her. Everyone went into the dining room and saw all the blue and they instantly knew I was pregnant with a boy. I handed the small box to Grams and she said, "I already know. You are pregnant and you are having a boy. This is so exciting. One of each". Charlie whispered to her. "Open the box Grams". She opened the box and gasped. "What the fuck? Are you kidding with me right now?" Steph and Joe wanted to know what was going on, so Charlie took the box and passed it down. There was silence and there was screaming. Even Joe was screaming. "HOLY SHIT, TWIN

BOYS? HOLY SHIT GUYS. THIS IS FUCKING AWESOME".
Grams was still sitting there saying, "What the fuck? Is this
a joke Meegs?" I assured her it was not a joke. "You will
have 2 more babies to hold for as long as you want". She
started crying. I told everyone that the twins were identical
and Charlie took the pictures out of his pocket and showed
Grams the winky dinks and she was laughing. "I love your
doctor Meegs. He is sweet and funny". Charlie was telling
everyone how he gave us his cell number in case we
needed him after hours or weekends". Joe said, "Now *that*
is a doctor. They don't make them like that anymore". So
we ate our Chinese food. Charlie chopped up the lo mein
noodles for Lizzie and I fed her. She was pretty good with
her spoon and fork now, but it was messy, so I fed her most
of the time. If she got cranky about it, I just let her do it and
cleaned up after. Steph said, she thought she would see
Lizzie wearing a t-shirt, but I told her that Charlie said after
the last pregnancy, we didn't want to do that this time. She
shook her head yes.

20

WELCOME TO THE WORLD

While we were still eating, Charlie called Angela and Mike. He looked at me and said, "My sister is gonna shit". Everyone was laughing at him. Angela answered in her usual way. "Hi Char, what's up? Everything ok?" Charlie said, "Yeah, everything is great. I just thought I would call and see how you guys are and find out what's going on?". She said, "Bullshit Char. What's going on? Tell me right Now". He said, "Well Meggie and I are pregnant again…". She interrupted by yelling. He had her on speaker. "OMG, THAT'S FANTASTIC…." Charlie interrupted her. "Well, there is just one thing though". She interrupted him. "What Char, What's happening, tell me Char or I will beat your ass when I see you". Charlie started laughing and everyone at the table was laughing. Charlie said, "You are not going to believe this, but Meggie and I are having identical twin boys". There was silence, like complete silence and we didn't know if she was still on the other end. "Ang? Are you there". Silence. "ANG, FUCKING ANSWER ME". She answered. "OMG GOD, CHAR. I DON'T KNOW WHAT TO SAY" We could hear her crying and Mike grabbed the phone. "Who is this?". Charlie told him and gave him the news. "Holy Shit Charlie, this is awesome news. The best news I've heard all day. When?" Charlie told him I was 4 months and that I probably would only carry them to 7 months. "So in about 3 months" We could still hear Angela crying in the background. Charlie took a picture of the babies in the box and the table with everything blue and sent it to Angela. She got back on the phone and she was still sobbing a little. "I'm sorry, I still can't believe this. Congratulations guys. I can't express how happy I am for you". I yelled. "I think we can guess how happy you are Ang". She yelled, "Congrats Meggie". I thanked her . She told Charlie that if we needed anything to let them know, including help and they would fly here to help.

As time went by, I swear I felt my stomach growing. They were both kicking the shit out of me. One kicked me under the ribs while I was eating and I stood up and spit my food all over the table. I scared Charlie. I told him what happened and apologized. "Please don't apologize for that." He just cleaned it up. I was 6 1/2 months and seeing the doctor every week now. I was humongous. I had to be careful walking. I had to wear sneakers in the house, but they were new ones and I didn't wear them outside. We never wore shoes in the house, but it was dangerous for me to wear just socks. The stairs were hardwood and downstairs was all tile. The bedrooms were hardwood and the bathrooms were all tile. Charlie followed me around like a puppy dog and took my arm as I went up and downstairs. I was a fucking blimp. No, actually I was bigger than a fucking blimp. I was a twin blimp. The doctor said I was doing good though and I was taking my vitamins everyday. I felt ok, I was just uncomfortable. I did a lot of sitting and Charlie was taking care of Lizzie. She was good baby. We never had any issues with her, but she was young yet. She was almost 2 years old. She was sweet and loving and laid back like Charlie and me. She was a sweetheart, an absolute sweetheart.

Now I was 7 1/2 and I was getting some contractions and Charlie called the doctor's office around 4:30 and they were closed. He texted the doctor on his personal phone and told him that I was having contractions but they were not at any certain times and he thought they were Braxton hicks. The doctor texted back and said to keep a close eye on how close they were and to notify him if there was any changes. I had one and then the next one would be 25 minutes later and then one would come 15 minutes and then it would be 30 minutes. They were all over the place. They were kicking like crazy. They want out and I wanted them out. We were relaxing in the living room and watching TV and Charlie had the news on. They were showing some robbery that happened a day ago and then on the screen we saw numbers on one of the houses. You guessed it. It was 3032. Charlie looked at me and I looked at him. He smiled. "I believe". I looked up the meaning on google and I quote, "Angel number 3032 is a powerful manifestation number that suggests growth and change are on the horizon. Trust in your creativity, intuition, and the potential of new beginnings to guide you on your journey towards greater spiritual connection and partnership". I read it to Charlie. He said, "Partnership, new beginnings, intuition". Yup, that's us right now".

"Ahhhhhhh, Woah, that was strong. Really strong". Charlie looked at the clock. He texted Steph and Joe. "Can you guys possibly come over and stay the night to watch Lizzie and Grams? Meggie is in labor and we may have to leave at a seconds notice". They both responded. They would be here in 10 minutes. I think Steph just left a bag packed for herself to come to my house. We counted on her so much. Joe too. They were always here to help. I told Charlie that we should leave them money in our wills and he agreed. "Ahhhh. OMG, that was bad". Charlie looked at me and said, "Meggie, that was only 5 minutes." I was just sitting there. In 5 minutes, another one came and it was stronger. Charlie texted the doctor and said, "Every 5 minutes". The doctor texted him back, "Get to the hospital now". Charlie got up and got my bag and his bag and went to the garage and put the bags in. Steph and Joe came and Charlie told him the contractions were 5 minutes apart and we were leaving. Lizzie was sleeping and Grams was in her room watching TV. We asked them to tell her and they did. We left. He helped me down the garage stairs and into the car and he buckled me in. He got in and we backed out of the garage and Steph and Joe were wishing us luck and they went back in. We got to the hospital and they had a wheelchair waiting for me. Charlie parked and got our bags out of the trunk and ran inside to find me. I was on my way to the maternity ward. He found me and he was out of breath. He must have been running. He held my hand. They put me in the hospital gown and I was freezing, so they gave me a heated blanket and Charlie put my socks on. He was rubbing my hands to warm them up. I had 2 contractions on the way up to the maternity ward. Now they were coming fast. Doctor Brewster was there waiting for me. He smiled and said, "I told you, you wouldn't make it the whole 9 months." Charlie asked him, "So will they be ok doc". He said, "They should be Charlie. They are healthy babies and they have a healthy mom. Let's get her in this room please" and he took my bed and started wheeling it towards a room. Charlie was holding my hand the whole time and staying right by my side. Once I was in the room, they gave me another warm blanket. I couldn't get warm. Charlie put another pair of socks on top of my other ones and he was rubbing my feet. The contractions were 2 minutes apart and I told the doctor I had to push. He told me not to. "Just try to wait ok?". He had his hand up there and then he smiled at me and said, "Ok, the next time you need to push, go for it". And it didn't take long. I pushed and Matthew Charles Hudson came into this world. He was 6lbs 2 oz, 19, inches and he had black hair. 10 minutes went by and then the contractions started again. Charlie was telling me I was doing a good job and he had tears coming down his cheeks. "He is beautiful Meggie. You can do this. One more". One last contraction and I pushed and Mason Charles Hudson was welcomed into this world. He was smaller than Matthew. He was only 5lbs 6 oz. He was 18 inches long and he had black hair too. They were both so small. I heard them both crying and it was a good sound. Charlie was kissing me. "You did it Meggie, You did it. I am so proud of you. Thank you Babe". He kissed every inch of my face. They asked him if he wanted to cut the cord and he said he did. One cord for identical twins. They put both babies on my chest and I could not believe how much they looked alike. Charlie laughed and said we would have to mark the bottom of their feet. A & B. "Charlie Hudson. You will not" and I laughed. I had to get stitches again and Charlie was kidding with the doctor. "Give her a honeymoon stitch doc". He looked at Charlie and said, "I already did". He laughed. I had 2 more beautiful babies. I looked at Charlie and said, "No more Charlie". He shook his head and said, "Nope this will do it". They were cleaning me up and the babies up and they wrapped them both in receiving blankets with blue hats and they looked like little burritos. They were so tiny. The pediatrician came in and looked them over and Mason didn't like it and was screaming bloody murder. The stethoscope was probably too cold for him. He stopped crying when the doctor was done. The doctor came to us and said they both look very healthy but they would check them over later. I was holding both babies, one in each arm and Charlie was over my shoulder and Dr. Brewster took our phones to take some pictures. We never told anyone the names that we picked. Not even Grams. We just picked them and that was it. And no one ever asked what they were. Then Charlie got to hold both babies. He had tears streaming down his face and the doctor took some pictures. I sent them to Steph, Joe, Grams and Angela and Mike. I sent the one of me with the babies and Charlie too. Our phones were going off like crazy. I attached all the pictures and texted. "Please welcome to this world, Matthew Charles Hudson, 6 lbs, 2 oz, 19inches and Mason Charles Hudson, 5 lbs 6 oz, 18 inches". The nurse asked me if I was breast feeding and I told her yes. She raised her eyebrows and said, "Are you sure honey?" I told her I was sure and that I was cow with my first one. She laughed and said, "Ok, if you say so". I would just pump a lot and fill the bottles so it would be easier and Charlie could help me feed them.

Steph texted me. "Megs, I love their names. I absolutely love them. More beautiful babies. They are so tiny. Congratulations, Hon". Charlie's sister got a flight and she was going to come by herself so she could help and I was happy about that. Really happy because we were gonna have our hands full. Steph said she would stay too. "I will stay in Grams room and Angela can use my bedroom."

The next morning was a little hectic. The nurses were in and out and I was trying to breastfeed. The nurse had me pumping already and filling bottles. I was getting ready for the onslaught of visitors that were going to come.

We ordered the cribs and dressers, 2 rocking chairs and a changing table for the boys rooms that matched what Ang and Mike sent us for Lizzie. Joe was at the house putting everything together. Steph brought Grams and Lizzie to see us and the new baby burritos. That was my nick name for them. I was going to call them burritos. Charlie just laughed at me and said, "Burrito #1 and Burrito #2. Matt will be #1 and Mason will be #2 ok?"

Steph, Lizzie and Grams walked into the room and the babies were with us in their basinets. Grams said, "OOOOHH, Meegs, They are so tiny. Oh my God, they are so cute. How do you feel Meegs?" I told her I was fine,

just sore. I laughed and said, "Meet Burrito #1 and #2."
She was laughing so hard. Steph peeked into the basinets
and she was holding Lizzie. "Lizzie, these are your new
brothers babe. Aren't they cute little burritos?" She looked
at me and laughed. Lizzie was calling them Beetos and
everyone started laughing. Charlie picked up Lizzie. "I
missed you so much my little cupcake". He was hugging
her and he showed her the babies again. He sat in the
chair with her in his lap and asked Steph to grab a burrito
and bring him over. Steph picked up Mason and brought
him over and put him in Lizzie's lap. "Be nice honey, they
are tiny babies." She was petting his hand and being so
gentle. I started tearing up. I hope it stays this way. Of
course, I know it won't but I am praying. I want them to all
get along.

Angela flew into the doorway and we were all surprised to
see her. I wasn't expecting her for a day or so. She came
right to me. "God Bless you sweetheart. Are you ok? Do
you need anything? Oh my god, they are beautiful." She
saw Charlie sitting in the chair with Lizzie and Mason and
started tearing up and leaned over to kiss Charlie and
Lizzie. "Congratulations to my baby brother. Look at you.
You are a natural". Hello Miss Lizzie." Steph took Mason
off Lizzie's lap and Angela picked up Lizzie. "You are a big
sister now. You have to help Mommy and Daddy now ok?".
Lizzie hugged her and kissed her. "You are such a cutie
pie". She continued to hold Lizzie and give her kisses.
Lizzie loved her Auntie Angela. Grams sat in a chair that
the nurse brought for her and Charlie handed her Burrito #1
(Matt). She was crying and she kept saying. "They are so

tiny. They are so beautiful. They look alike Charlie. Oh my God, I love them so much". Charlie told Grams that they were identical twins. "They are supposed to look like each other Grams". She didn't understand, but eventually she would. Grams was in heaven. Charlie said to her, "Now you can take your pick of babies to hold". Lizzie went to Grams and said, "MY GAMMA". Grams told her that she was her favorite girl and always would be. Lizzie leaned into Grams and was hugging her arm. Charlie looked at her and said, "They are gonna fight over you Grams". She smiled up at him. Angela saw me trying to stay awake and said, "You guys, we should go back to the house and let these guys get some rest. They will probably be coming home tomorrow." Everyone got their stuff and they were saying their goodbyes. Charlie said, "Steph, if Joe comes later, can you ask him to bring the 2 car seats from the boys room?" She said she would take care of it. Charlie added, "And Fucking food. I am starving". He handed her $40. "Please get us some food." Joe came about an hour later, with the carseats and a bunch of food from MacDonalds. Charlie and I were eating like we haven't eaten in ages. The food at the hospital was terrible. Charlie had 2 burgers, fries and his chocolate shake and I had the crispy chicken sandwich, Fries and a chocolate shake. OMG. When you are hungry like that, everything tastes so good, except for hospital food. LOL. It was time for feeding, so the nurse handed Matt to Charlie and gave him a bottle of my milk and she handed me Mason, so I could breastfeed him. They both had good appetites. Mason was really going to town. Charlie changed Matt and the nurse changed Mason and they were all burped and wrapped up like little burritos again. They were put back into the basinets. I pumped some more milk for the next feeding and I was told that both burritos were going to be circumcised in a couple of hours and that we were all going home tomorrow. I needed a nap. I was so tired I could hardly keep my eyes open. The nurse helped me to the bathroom and then I took a 2 hour nap but they woke me up to take my blood pressure and take my blood. Doc Brewster came in and told me I needed to keep taking those vitamins because my levels were very low. "Otherwise, everything looks good. I will see you in 4 weeks, unless you have any problems. You have my number. Congratulations guys". The babies were circumcised and everything went well.

Charlie went out to get us some food for dinner. I told him that Italian or Chinese would be fine for me. He said, "I was thinking Chinese. I will get your usual". I took a small nap while he was gone. When he got back, we started eating, but our little burritos were hungry, so we stopped to do their feeding. This time I breast fed Matt and Charlie took Mason. We ate when they were done, changed and burped. I pumped more milk for the next feeding when I was done eating. This was going to be my life for the next few months. Pumping, feeding, changing diapers, burping and eating cold dinners, but it was all worth it and I had a lot of help at home.

The next day, we got the babies dressed up in the outfits we bought them. They had onesies with bowties. We wrapped them part way in the receiving blankets. The nurse wheeled me down in the wheelchair and I had Mason in my lap. Charlie took all the flowers and gifts down earlier with Mason's carseat. He had Matt in his car seat and he carried him. We had to plan all this ahead of time. He had the car pulled up front. He put Matt in the car and then he took Mason and put him in his car seat. He had moved Lizzie's car seat to the middle of the seat. Then I got up and got in the front seat. Charlie laughed and said, "We need a bus". The nurse congratulated us and wished us luck. "You are gonna need it. You guys have your hands full". Charlie told her we had a lot of help at home.

We arrived home and Charlie pulled into the garage. Steph and Joe met us in the garage to help. They each grabbed a baby from the backseat and Charlie helped me into the house. Charlie said, "Thanks Guys. This helps a lot". The basinets were set up in the sitting room and they were transferred to them. Lizzie came running to me. "Mommy, Mommy". I couldn't pick her up, so I sat in the chair and she sat in my lap and we were hugging and I was kissing her. "I missed you my little cupcake. I love you so much. Were you a good girl for Steph and Grams?" She shook her head and said yes. Steph told me she was a very good girl. Grams came out to welcome us home and see the babies. They were sleeping so she didn't ask to hold them, but we knew she wanted to, so Charlie promised her that she could feed one when they were ready. She was so excited. I went in the bathroom to pump more milk. I had so much and I was so swollen. I was filling bottles like crazy. Charlie brought me a folding chair so I could sit and pump. I told him, "OMG, I have so much, I can't keep up with it." He brought me more bottles. He kept up with cleaning and sterilizing them. The housekeeper, Lynne was there cleaning up and she asked Charlie if there was anything extra she could do to help. Charlie couldn't think of anything off the top of his head, but she told him that if we needed any help with the babies or whatever, we could call her. "You have my cell number. Don't hesitate to call me". He thanked her for that. "Nice to know. Thank you".

Angela stayed for a week and was a huge help. She cooked, did laundry, helped to feed, change, bathe, burp, rock. She was awesome. Steph stayed for 2 weeks and offered more, but Charlie told her to get back to her life. We had a nice dinner with everyone before they all left. Lizzie got upset when her Auntie Angela left and when Steph was walking out with her suitcase. They both told her they would be back to visit. She cried and ran to her Grammie. Grams held her and comforted her and then she ran to her Daddy for more attention. We made sure she got a lot of attention and that nothing changed for her, just because we had extra babies to take care of. She was my number one priority and she knew it and she had us wrapped around her pinky. She was a girly girl and knew how to get us to feel bad for her. But I have to say that she was really good with her new brothers and she wanted to help, so we let her. We let her hold them one at a time so she would feel important and needed. Grams was in her glory. She loved every minute of every day. She held the babies and loved on Lizzy all day.

We did take out for a few weeks until we were on a schedule and then I started making dinners again. I usually made a few big casseroles in a row and then we would eat leftovers so I didn't have to cook everyday. Charlie knew I was tired and he helped all the time. He did laundry and helped me cook and fed babies and changed diapers.

Charlie was a happy man. He had a beautiful little girl that he called Cupcake and he adored her and twin boys that he adored and loved with all his heart and soul. He truly loved these children with all his heart and they loved him back. He spoiled them rotten and bought them anything their heart desired, within reason of course. He would do anything for them.

They were all attached to their mommy too. I had a special connection (bond) with each one of them. I think every mother has a special connection with their children. It's hard to describe, but once you have a child, you will understand what I am talking about. I don't know if it's a feeling you have, if it's love or if it's built in to you when you give birth to them, but it's there. I hope you all get to experience it because it is the best feeling ever.

Grams lived to be 90 years old and it was a very sad day when she left us. But I felt good that she was able to meet and play with her great grandchildren. I gave her everything she needed and we cared for her till the end. She lived a long and awesome life and we made sure of that.

Steph and Joe got married and they had 2 girls and one boy. Grams left both of them money in her will. Enough so that they would be very comfortable and I was so happy about that. They were always there for her and us.

Lizzie and the Burritos got along all the time. That dream came true for me. They were all very close. Did they fight? Yes, of course they did, but they loved each other and 98% of the time, they got along. They all played together. They were all good kids. They were loving, caring and well behaved. That is all you can ask for as a parent.

Charlie and I, are and always will be in love, for the rest of our lives. He is always good to me. He never yells or swears at me. He treats me like a queen and I love him with all my heart and soul. I still get tingles down to my toes when he kisses me. He is an awesome Daddy and husband and his children are his everything.

3032

"Angel number 3032 is a powerful manifestation number that suggests growth and change are on the horizon.

 Trust in your creativity, intuition, and the potential of new beginnings to guide you on your journey towards greater spiritual connection and partnership."

Taken from astrology.com

THANK YOU CHRISTINE TUCCI